Accounting and Budgeting

S Bashir and D Morgan

Croner Publications Ltd
Croner House
London Road
Kingston upon Thames
Surrey KT2 6SR
Tel: 0181-547 3333

D1149955

Copyright © 1997 Croner Publications Ltd
First published 1997

Published by
Croner Publications Ltd
Croner House
London Road
Kingston upon Thames
Surrey KT2 6SR
Tel: 0181-547 3333

While every care has been taken
in the writing and editing of this book,
readers should be aware that only Acts of Parliament
and Statutory Instruments have the force of law,
and that only the courts can authoritatively
interpret the law.

British Library Cataloguing-in-Publication Data.
A catalogue record for this book is available
from the British Library.

ISBN 1 85524 395 4

Printed by Whitstable Litho Printers Ltd, Whitstable, Kent.

THE AUTHORS

Sabahat Bashir ACCA is a qualified accountant with eight years commercial experience in public practice. She currently lectures in accountancy and business studies.

David Morgan MSc has had extensive manufacturing, service, government and consultancy experience. For the past 10 years he has lectured in management and accounting practice both in this country and abroad.

INTRODUCTION

The aim of *Accounting and Budgeting* is to deepen the layperson's understanding of basic accounting principles. This book gives clear explanations of accounting practices and attempts to show how accounting and budgeting affects management decision making.

The book will prove invaluable to anyone requiring information about budgeting, whatever their role and whatever type of company they work for.

CONTENTS

CHAPTER ONE

FINANCIAL ACCOUNTING

WHAT ARE ACCOUNTS?

Accountants prepare different types of accounts depending on the information needed. The two main types are as follows.

1. *Financial accounting* — which centres on showing how a business has performed financially. A set of financial accounts is primarily a summary of financial transactions of a business over a period of time (usually a year). A financial accountant will produce both the profit and loss account and the balance sheet. The profit and loss account measures the amount of profit or loss made over the time period. The balance sheet summarises the financial position of the business at the end of the time period.

2. *Management accounting* — which concentrates on giving financial information to managers and is largely concerned with business planning, control and decision-making. A management accountant will prepare things like cash flow forecasts and budgets, and will provide information on, for example, the cost of launching a new product. The data produced by a management accountant will be used internally by managers.

HOW ARE FINANCIAL ACCOUNTS PREPARED?

A business collects various documents relating to its financial transactions, eg sales invoices, credit notes, bank statements. The information contained in such documents is used to record the financial transactions of the business. The process of recording is called bookkeeping and may consist of either handwritten or computerised records (or a mixture of both). Once recorded, these transactions can then be summarised and a picture built up of what has happened in the business over the time period required. The profit and loss account and the balance sheet are produced from the summarised transactions.

TYPES OF BUSINESS ORGANISATION

The way a business is run depends largely on what legal category it falls into. In the UK, the three main forms of organisation are:

- sole traders
- partnerships
- limited companies.

A *sole trader* is an individual person running a business for his or her own benefit. There is no distinction between the sole trader and the business, ie the business is owned by the sole trader. This means that not only can he or she take all the profits but also has to suffer any losses made. It also means that he or she is personally responsible for all of the debts of the business.

In a *partnership*, two or more people operate a business. Each person involved in running the business is called a partner. The partners own and manage the business between them. The profits and losses may be shared equally but are often divided in relation to the amount of time or money a partner has put into the business. The partners are each personally responsible for the debts of the business. This is known as joint and general liability.

A *limited company* is a legal being in its own right, separate from its owners. This is a very important distinction as it means that the owners (called shareholders) cannot in general be held personally responsible for the debts of the business, as is the case for sole traders and partnerships, unless personal guarantees have been given.

WHO USES FINANCIAL ACCOUNTS?

There are many people to whom the financial accounts of an organisation are of interest.

1. The *owners or shareholders* who use accounts to check that the business is financially healthy and that they are getting a good return on the money they have put into the business.
2. The *management* can use them to assess their own performance.
3. *Banks and other lenders* are interested in the ability of the business to meet interest charges and repay whatever money has been lent.
4. *HM Customs & Excise* and *The Inland Revenue* try to make sure that the right amount of VAT and taxes on profits are paid.
5. *Creditors* (people the business owes money to), like the banks, want to ensure that they will get paid on time.
6. The *employees* are likely to be concerned about the longer term prospects of the business as this is directly linked to job security.
7. *Potential investors* use accounts to see whether or not they should put their money into the business.
8. Leasing/hire purchase companies.

ACCOUNTING PRINCIPLES

ACCOUNTING STANDARDS

Accounting standards are set in order to give guidance on various accounting issues, for example, how to treat stocks and work-in-progress when preparing accounts. The purpose of such guidelines is to achieve acceptable standards in the preparation and presentation of financial accounts.

Accounting standards take the form of documents called Statements of Standard Accounting Practice (SSAPs) and Financial Reporting Standards (FRSs).

SSAPs were issued by the Accounting Standards Committee (ASC) and were revised and sometimes withdrawn over the years as they underwent updating or became obsolete. The ASC was replaced in 1991 by the Accounting Standards Board (ASB). The ASB adopted the existing SSAPs but has also gone on to issue its own standards — FRSs.

Using the standards should lead to the consistent treatment of similar transactions in different businesses. The standards also detail information which must be shown in the accounts. Although accounting standards have no legal standing, all members of the professional accountancy bodies (eg chartered accountants) are expected to observe them. If a standard is not followed this must be explained in the accounts.

ACCOUNTING CONCEPTS

As well as accounting standards, there are also various accounting concepts. These are the assumptions that are used when preparing financial accounts. The main ones are listed below:

- going concern
- consistency
- prudence
- accruals
- profit recognition
- materiality
- historic cost
- monetary measurement.

Going Concern

This means the accounts have been prepared on the basis that the business is going to continue for the forseeable future and is not expecting to be wound up or liquidated. When a business is being wound up, many of the items in the balance sheet are likely to realise considerably less than values in the balance sheet on a going concern basis.

Consistency

Business transactions must be treated in a consistent way over an accounting period and from one period to the next otherwise comparisons become meaningless. An example of this would be applying the same rate of wear and tear (depreciation) to the company vehicles from one year to the next.

Prudence

Revenues are only included in the accounts when it is reasonably certain that the cash will be received (eg if it is known that a customer will not pay) then the corresponding sale should not be included in the accounts. Coupled with this, all possible costs that are likely to be incurred in the accounting period should be included in the accounts, even if there is a chance that the costs will not have to be paid. This has the overall effect of not anticipating profits which may never materialise.

Accruals

This is also known as the matching concept. It means that the costs included in the accounts should reflect what has actually been used up rather than what has just been paid for. For example, a gas bill which is received quarterly by the business is unlikely to be a bill which matches the accounting year end. Suppose a bill is received for gas used to the end of November and the accounting period end is December. Gas will still have been used during December even though a bill will not be received until March. Using the accruals concept, an amount will be included in the accounts to December to reflect the gas used but not yet paid for. Similarly, costs that have been paid for in advance, such as insurance, will be taken out of the accounts. With sales figures all the sales that have been made are included, rather than the cash received for them. This treatment has the advantage of matching sales revenue with cost of sales and thus enabling calculation of an accurate profit margin.

Profit Recognition

This looks at when a sale should be included in the accounts. Many businesses make both cash and credit sales. There is no problem with cash sales. When goods are sold for cash, the date of sale is the date the cash is received. When a credit sale is made there is a delay between the customer receiving and paying for the goods. There are various stages in a credit sale:
- the customer places an order and receives the goods
- an invoice is sent to the customer
- the customer pays for the goods.

When should the sale be included in the accounts? It could be argued that a sale occurs when the customer receives goods. However, many businesses send invoices after goods have been despatched and it is usual practice to recognise a sale at the invoice date. By this stage the transaction between the business and its customer has been formalised and the customer is legally obliged to pay for the goods. The profit recognition concept includes credit sales in the accounts at the point they are invoiced, this is usually before the cash is received.

Materiality

If an item in the accounts is of insignificant value to affect the accounts overall it is considered immaterial. The accounting treatment of transactions can depend on whether they are considered significant (material) or not. An example of this would be including in the accounts a sale that had not yet been invoiced — this is not usual accounting practice. If the value of the sale is £10 and the overall sales for the period are £100,000, the £10 sale is not material and it does not really matter if the sale is included or not. If, however, an uninvoiced sale of £20,000 was included in the accounts, this would be material and it should be taken out.

Historic Cost

The value of items in accounts is shown as the actual cost of the item at the time of the transaction, rather than someone's opinion of what it is currently worth. There are certain exceptions to this, the main one being that property can be shown at its current value.

Monetary Measurement

Only things that can be measured in terms of money are included in the accounts. Good staff morale in a business could not be included in the accounts.

It should be noted that in applying these accounting standards and concepts, there is still a degree of individual judgment. It is quite possible for two people to produce two different sets of accounts using the same business records.

RECORDING TRANSACTIONS

WHY RECORD TRANSACTIONS?

Every trading business generates transactions. Every time something is bought or sold by a business at least one transaction will have taken place. A simple example is a newsagent selling a paper. If the newsagent did not keep a record of such transactions, it would be impossible to know how much income he or she is receiving. If the income is not known, it is also not possible to measure the profit or loss the business is making, ie the newsagent will not know how the business is doing. In order to gauge the financial performance of a business it is vital that a record is kept of its transactions. In the example above, the newsagent would probably record the transaction by ringing up a sale on the cash register. At the end of the day, the cash register will be able to print off a list of all the sales that have been entered that day. The list is printed on the till roll and the total at the bottom shows the amount of sales made that day. The till roll only records the monetary part of the day's transactions, ie how much money the day's sales have brought in. Generally, it is the monetary aspect of business transactions that accountants are interested in.

SOURCE DATA

The transactions that occur as a result of trading produce various documents, the newsagents till roll being an example. These documents are often referred to as source data. The source data is used to write up the books of account, ie the accounting records. The accounting records are then used to prepare financial accounts — mainly the profit and loss account and the balance sheet. Other examples of source data are:

- cheque counterfoils
- purchase invoices
- copy sales invoices
- credit notes

- petty cash vouchers
- banking records (eg paying in books)
- wages records.

It should be remembered that not all businesses will generate all of these types of documents. The newsagent will not issue sales invoices to all customers. The source data produced depends on the type of business activity.

BOOKS OF ACCOUNT

The nature of accounting records varies greatly between businesses depending largely on the size, structure and type of business activity. It is possible to identify basic records which most businesses keep in one form or another. Nearly all businesses buy and sell, and have a bank account. Basic accounting records therefore keep a track of what has been bought and sold, and what has gone through the bank account. Such records are often called the books of prime entry, because they are the point at which the businesses transactions first enter the recording system.

The books of prime entry may be handwritten books or entered onto a computer and stored as disks. Many small businesses use a combination of both manual and computerised records. The main ones are:

- the cash book
- the day books.

The Cash Book

The cash book is primarily used to record bank transactions, although some cash books record both bank and cash transactions. Maintaining the books of account (bookkeeping) has been in existence for many hundreds of years. Before the advent of banks, business transactions had to be done in cash, hence the term "cash book". Today, although most business transactions go through the bank account, the name for the cash book has stayed the same. Figure 1 shows an extract from a typical handwritten cash book.

Figure 1 — Cash Book Extract

Receipts			Payments					
Details	Date	Bank (£)	Details	Date	Bank (£)	Ref	Rent (£)	Wages (£)
Sales	4/7/97	1000	A Smith	3/7/97	500	001	500	
Sales	7/7/97	1000	B Jones	5/7/97	1000	002		1000

Receipts (ie cash or cheques paid into the bank) are entered on the left-hand side, along with the date, details and a reference if needed. Payments (ie cheques issued) are recorded on the right-hand side also with the date, details and reference (often the cheque number). The payments side is extended to allow for analysis of the expenditure.

If cash transactions also need to be recorded in the cash book then an extra column headed *cash* is simply added on both the receipts and payments sides alongside the *bank* column. The bank and cash transactions will then be entered under the appropriate headings.

The cash book can be used to see exactly what the business's bank balance is at, say, the end of a week or month. Using Figure 1, suppose that these are the only transactions for the week and that the bank account has just been opened (so that the balance on the account before these transactions is nil). First, total the *bank* columns. This gives £2000 for receipts and £1500 for payments. Second, under the *totals* add a figure to one side which will make the *totals* the same — in this case £500 is added under the payments total. The £500 is the "balance carried down".

The cash book is then ruled off for both sides and the balance carried down is entered on the opposite side of the cash book, under the ruled off *total*. In this example, the £500 will be entered on the receipts side under the total of £2000. It is now called the "balance brought forward". As it is on the receipts side it means that there is £500 in the bank at the end of the week. The whole procedure is known as "balancing the cash book".

Figure 2 — Cash Book Balance

Receipts			Payments					
Details	Date	Bank (£)	Details	Date	Bank (£)	Ref	Rent (£)	Wages (£)
Sales	4/7/97	1000	A Smith	3/7/97	500	001	500	
Sales	7/7/97	1000	B Jones	5/7/97	1000	002		1000
Total		2000	**Total**		1500			
Balance b/f 8/7		500	Balance c/f 7/7		500			

Small amounts of cash are usually recorded in a petty cash book. The petty cash book will also have receipts and payments sides similar to the main cash book. The amounts entered on the receipts side will be the cash drawn from the bank or taken from cash sales. The payments made from this cash are entered on the payments side. The petty cash book can be balanced in the same way as the main cash book.

It is essential that every time a bank statement is received the individual items are checked off against the corresponding items in the cash book and that the balance recorded on the statement, adjusted for cheques that have not been presented and for amounts paid in that have not been credited, is agreed to the cash book balance. This is known as a bank reconciliation.

The Day Books

Day books are used to record sales and purchases. They tend to be used in businesses where there are credit transactions. Many businesses make sales on credit, ie there is an agreed delay between the customer receiving the goods and paying for them. Similarly, the business will receive goods from its suppliers before they have been paid for. Due to the accounting concept "profit recognition", it is invoiced sales that are included in the accounts, rather than the actual cash received. For a business that makes credit sales the invoiced sales figure will be different to the cash received for a given time period. It is therefore necessary to keep a record of invoiced sales, and also of invoices received for goods bought. This is done via the day books, separate ones being maintained for sales and purchases, and may also be kept for sales credit notes and purchase returns.

The day books are simply a list of invoices. All sales invoices issued by the business will be entered into the sales day book. Details such as the invoice date and amount, and the customer name will be recorded. At regular intervals, usually weekly or monthly, the invoices are totalled to give sales over a period. The purchases day book lists similar information except that details of invoices received are entered.

As with the cash book, day books can be maintained either manually or on a computer.

TYPES OF BOOKKEEPING SYSTEMS

Bookkeeping can be done on a single or double entry basis, although the most widely used by far is the double entry system.

SINGLE ENTRY

This method is really only used by some small businesses, usually because the time, resources or expertise are not available to maintain a full double entry system. A typical set of single entry records could include a cash book, bank statements and the owner's estimate of what is owed and what is owing. Single entry is literally when only one entry is made into the books of account for each transaction that takes place. An example of this is entering a payment made for goods bought on credit into the cash book — this being the only entry that is made in the records. It is not possible to produce a profit and loss account and a balance sheet from single entry systems. What usually happens in practice is that the accountant for the business will reconstruct the information needed and this necessarily involves using double entry techniques.

DOUBLE ENTRY

Double entry bookkeeping involves recording the dual nature of financial transactions — so for every transaction two entries are made in the accounting records. Consider cash received from a sale, the cash has increased and it has also made a sale. The two entries (the double entry that would be made) would be to record the cash received and the sale made. Each entry is recorded in a designated account. An account is simply a record of the transactions that have taken place under that particular heading. In the example above, an entry would be made in the cash account and an entry also made in the sales account. Over a period of time the transactions in each account accumulate. The accumulated entries in these accounts are used to prepare the financial accounts. Remember that an account is basically a storage location — entries for similar transactions are recorded in the same account.

The various accounts can be maintained either manually or on computer (as is increasingly the case). A ledger is a series of accounts. The main ledgers kept are:

- the nominal ledger
- the sales ledger
- the purchase (bought) ledger.

The *nominal ledger* includes all the accounts that are kept by the business, and is used to produce the financial accounts, ie the profit and loss account and the balance sheet. Examples of the accounts kept in this ledger are sales, purchases, bank, wages, etc.

The *sales ledger* is used to record how much individual customers owe the business. Each customer has an account. Totalling all of the sales ledger accounts gives the overall amount the business is owed by its customers. There is no need to keep a sales ledger if the business only has cash sales.

The *purchase ledger* (sometimes called the bought ledger) records the amounts the business owes to its suppliers. As with the sales ledger, each supplier has an account. Adding up all the individual accounts in the purchase ledger gives the total amount the business owes to its suppliers.

In theory, there is nothing to stop all the customer and supplier accounts being entered individually into the nominal ledger, rather than being kept in separate sales and purchase ledgers. Indeed, this may well be the case when there are very few customers and suppliers involving sales and purchases on credit. However, on a practical level, it makes sense to maintain sales and purchase ledgers when there are many credit transactions. It also makes it easier to see the totals, owed and owing, by customers and to suppliers respectively.

Double Entry Method

Double entry involves making two entries into the system. The two entries are called the debit entry and the credit entry. The debit and credit in each transaction recorded must be equal amounts. In the UK, the convention is to use the left-hand side of accounts for debits and the right-hand side for credits (see below).

Customer Account

£	£
Debit (dr)	Credit (cr)

The golden rule of double entry is that "for every debit there must be a credit", ie for every debit entered in an account there must also be a credit entry of equal amount in another account. It is also advisable to enter the date of the transaction and to cross-reference the accounts. Debits and credits are also opposite. This means that if an account ends up with exactly the same amount of debits as there are credits, they cancel each other out and the net effect is nil.

Example

Consider the following transactions that take place on a particular day.

1. A filing cabinet is bought for £200 cash.
2. The £100 telephone bill is paid for by cheque.
3. A customer buys goods worth £500 on credit.

How are these transactions recorded using the double entry system?

In the first transaction, cash has been used so the amount of cash held has gone down by £200, which has been spent on a filing cabinet. The two accounts involved are therefore the cash account and the filing cabinet account. Payments made by cash or cheque are recorded on the credit side of the cash or bank account. This means that receipts (money paid into the bank or cash accounts) is recorded as a debit. If the cash account has to be credited with the £200, then the corresponding £200 debit entry must be made in the filing cabinet account. The debit (dr) and credit (cr) entries can be shown as follows.

Transaction 1

Dr	Filing cabinet account	£200
Cr	Cash account	£200

Figure 3 shows how this transaction is recorded in the above accounts.

Figure 3 — Double Entry for a Cash Payment

Filing Cabinet Account			
	£		£
1/8/97 Cash a/c	200		

Cash Account			
	£		£
		1/8/97 Filing cabinet a/c	200

In the second transaction, the two accounts affected are the telephone account and the bank account. As in the first transaction, the payment made out of the bank is entered on the credit side of the bank account. The debit entry can only then be made in the telephone account.

Transaction 2

Dr	Telephone account	£100
Cr	Bank account	£100

Figure 4 shows the entries as they would appear in these accounts.

Figure 4 — Double Entry for a Bank Payment

Telephone Account			
	£		£
1/8/97 Bank a/c	100		

Bank Account		
£		£
	1/8/97 Telephone a/c	100

Note: Remember that crediting the bank/cash accounts when payments are made is simply a convention when using double entry. It has absolutely nothing to do with the everyday meaning of the word "credit" and should not be confused with standard banking terminology, which uses crediting an account to mean that money has been paid in.

In the third transaction, a sale of £500 has been made, so the sales account has been affected. As this is a credit sale, however, the £500 has not yet been received, so the transaction has not involved the bank or cash accounts. The £500 is owed by the customer and this is recorded in the customer's individual account. Again, using double entry convention, sales are recorded on the credit side of the sales account. This then leaves the customer's account to be the debit entry.

Transaction 3

Dr	Customer account	£500
Cr	Sales account	£500

Figure 5 shows this transaction entered into the customer's and sales accounts.

Figure 5 — Double Entry for a Credit Transaction

Customer Account		
	£	£
1/8/97 Sales a/c	500	

Sales Account		
	£	£
	1/8/97 Customer a/c	500

What happens when the customer pays the £500? Now the bank account has been affected and the other account involved is the customer's account. Bank receipts are recorded as debit entries, so the credit entry must be made on the customer's account. The customer's account now has both a debit entry of £500 and also a credit entry of £500. As the amounts are equal, the debit and the credit cancel each other out and the customer's account will show that no money is owing, which is of course the correct position.

When goods are bought on credit, the double entry would be to debit the purchases account and to credit the supplier's account. This is the reverse to the entries made for the credit sale above. When the supplier is paid, eg by cheque, the entries made are to debit the supplier's account (thus cancelling out the earlier credit) and credit the bank account.

Using a Cash Book and Day Books

Suppose the cash book is used only to record bank transactions and is written up on a weekly basis. At the end of the week, the receipts and payments are totalled. These totals are then posted (entered) into the bank account in the nominal ledger (this is the ledger which contains all of the accounts kept by the business). The receipts total is entered on the debit side and the payments total on the credit side of the bank account in the nominal ledger. In this particular week, all of the bank receipts are sales made and all of the payments are for wages. To complete the double entry, the sales account is credited with the same amount as for bank receipts (debit bank account £X, credit sales account £X). The wages account is debited with the same amount as for bank payments (debit wages account £Y, credit bank account £Y). From this simple example, it can be seen that one advantage of keeping a cash book is that rather than entering every single bank transaction into the nominal ledger using many double entries, a series of transactions have been entered using only two sets of double entry.

The day books can be used to similar effect. The periodic (eg weekly or monthly) totals from, for example the sales day book are posted to the credit side on the sales account in the nominal ledger. The other side of the double entry is to debit the various sales ledger accounts, ie the customers accounts. The sales account is credited with one total. The customer accounts are debited with various amounts but the overall debits must add up to the same amount as the total that has been credited to the sales account, if double entry principles are followed.

ACCOUNT BALANCES

The balance on an account is the difference between the total debits and the total credits entered on the account. Figure 6 shows an account with various entries.

Figure 6 — Account Balance

Customer Account			
	£		£
9/11/97 Cash a/c	1000	18/10/97 Bank a/c	250
5/11/97 Cash a/c	500		

The debits add up to £1500 and the credit is £250. The account balance is: £1500 – £250 = £1250. As the debit total is larger than the credit total, the £1250 is a debit balance. If the figures are reversed, giving credits of £1500 and a debit of £250, the account balance becomes £1250 credit.

TRIAL BALANCE

At the end of an accounting period, all the balances on the accounts are listed. The total debit balances should exactly equal the total credit balances. The trial balance is taken out to check that both sides of each double entry have been recorded. Although a trial balance that balances, ie the debits equal the credits, shows that for every debit an equal credit has been entered, it cannot reveal debits/credits entered onto wrong accounts. It also cannot identify a double entry where the debit has been mistakenly entered on the credit side and the credit on the debit side. In practice, however, accountants are usually able to get the trial balance to balance as there are numerous checks and ways to locate and correct errors. Using the three transactions listed in *Double Entry Method* earlier, taking out a trial balance gives the following.

Figure 7 — Trial Balance

	Debit (£)	Credit (£)
Filing cabinet account	200	
Cash account		200
Telephone account	100	
Bank account		100
Customer account	500	
Sales account		500
Total	<u>800</u>	<u>800</u>

The trial balance is used to prepare the profit and loss account and the balance sheet. Before this can be done, adjustments may have to be made in order that accounting standards and concepts are met, for example accruals can be incorporated at this stage.

After the adjustments have been done, the trial balance should contain all the information necessary to produce the profit and loss account and the balance sheet. This is done by sorting the account balances under these two headings, eg the sales account balance is part of the profit and loss account, while the bank account balance comes under the balance sheet.

The profit and loss account contains items relating to income and expenditure. The balance sheet consists of items that are called *assets*, *liabilities* and anything relating to *capital*. Assets are things that are owned by the business, eg buildings, machinery, etc which are termed *fixed assets*. *Current assets* include stocks, work in progress, cash and bank balances and debtors. Liabilities are amounts owing by the business, eg bank overdraft loans and creditors. The difference between total assets and total liabilities is the "net worth" of the business and is represented by the firms "capital", which could be said to be funds *put* into the business, together with accumulated profits and reserves. The capital introduced may be a sole trader's personal savings used to set up a business or money raised by a limited company from issuing shares.

A journal is a form of double entry. It consits of a debit and credit entry together with the date and a description (narrative) of what the transaction relates to. The use of journals is particularly important in computerised systems as all the transactions are input using journals.

THE PROFIT AND LOSS ACCOUNT

WHAT IS A PROFIT AND LOSS ACCOUNT?

The profit and loss account (P & L) is one of the financial statements that is produced from the trial balance. It measures financial performance over a period of time and gives the amount of profit or loss made over that period.

The accountant's meaning of the term "profit" has little to do with cash except in very simple terms. If some goods are bought for cash today for £100 and sold tomorrow for £200 cash then a £100 "profit" is made in cash. If, however, the same goods are bought and sold for the same amounts but on credit, the cash position is unchanged but a "profit" has still been made as far as the accountant is concerned. There has been a sale of £200 and the cost of the goods needed in making that sale (the cost of the sale) is £100. The profit is the difference between the two figures, ie £100, so profit can be said to be sales minus the cost of sales.

	£
Sales	200
Less cost of sales	100
Profit	<u>100</u>

In reality there are usually other costs involved when running a business, such as rent and wages. These are also taken into account when measuring profit. The profit and loss account then looks as follows.

	£
Trading account	
Sales	200
Less cost of sales	<u>100</u>
Gross profit	<u>100</u>
Profit and loss account	
Less expenses	<u>50</u>
Net profit	<u>50</u>

Gross profit is the term given to the profit made from sales when only the costs directly associated with buying or making the goods sold are taken into account. Net profit is the profit made from sales after all costs have been taken off. Net profit is sometimes referred to as the "bottom line" figure. Gross profit depends directly on the amount of sales made — the higher the sales, the greater the amount of gross profit. Net profit takes account of other costs (expenses) often called "overheads". Expenses tend to stay the same regardless of the amount of sales so the net profit is not directly affected by sales in the same way as gross profit is.

It should be remembered that in preparing the profit and loss account, all the various accounting standards and concepts have to be observed. One of the main ones is the accruals or matching concept. The amounts shown in the profit and loss account should reflect what has actually been used up over the period. A consequence of this is that if a business has stocks of goods unsold at the end of the year, they must not be included in the cost of sales figure, as they obviously have not been part of the cost of any sales made in the period. Similarly, any stocks of goods available at the start of the time period should be included in the cost of sales figure. The cost of sales figure is worked out as follows.

	£
Add cost of opening stocks	100
Add cost of goods bought	150
Less cost of closing stocks	150
Equals cost of goods sold	100

On the profit and loss account itself, the cost of sales figures is presented as follows.

	£	£
Opening stock	100	
Add purchases	150	
	250	
Less closing stock	150	100

The accruals concept is also applied to expenses. The main types of expenses that often need to be adjusted are items such as telephone, gas, electricity, rent, rates and insurance. If something has been paid for in advance, eg insurance, the amount that does not relate to the period is taken out of the profit and loss account. When things like gas and electricity have been used in the period but the bill not due to be received till after the time period, the amount used is estimated and added to the profit and loss account figures.

Another main accounting concept followed is that of profit recognition. This is the practice of including all sales in the profit and loss account that have been invoiced, regardless of whether the cash has been received.

SOLE TRADERS AND PROFIT AND LOSS ACCOUNTS

The way in which a sole trader or a partnership would usually present a profit and loss account (P & L) is shown below. Please note that the precise format will depend on the type of business, eg a sole trader who provides services rather than buys and sells goods will not need a "cost of sales" heading. The format below, however, is widely used as it is suitable for many types of business activity.

Figure 8 — J Smith Limited
Trading and Profit and Loss Account (Year End 31-12-X7)

	£000s	£000s
Sales		200
Cost of sales		
Add opening stock	100	
Add purchases	150	
	250	
Less closing stock	150	100
Gross profit		100
Less expenses		50
Net profit		50

Note: In practice the expenses are listed out under various headings, eg wages, rent, telephone.

LIMITED COMPANIES AND PROFIT AND LOSS ACCOUNTS

The profit and loss account (P & L) of a limited company is prepared using the same accounting principles as that of a sole trader or a partnership but an additional section called the appropriation account is produced. This comes under the net profit line and shows what has been taken (appropriated) from the net profit. Limited companies also have certain legal obligations in relation to the profit and loss account (and the financial accounts in general).

UK companies are required by law to publish (make publicly available) annual accounts. These are "external" accounts and accounts prepared for use within the company are "internal" accounts. The profit and loss account format is similar to that of the sole trader/partnership, with the appropriation account added.

The appropriation account shows the following deductions from net profit:

- corporation tax charge
- dividends
- transfers to reserves
- retained profits.

Corporation Tax

This is a tax paid only by companies. At the time the accounts are prepared, the exact amount of tax to be paid is unlikely to be known, therefore the figure in the profit and loss account will usually contain an estimate.

Dividends

These are paid to shareholders (the owners) of the company. They represent the return on the investment made by the shareholder and can only be paid if there are enough profits. Dividends are often paid during the year since many companies produce interim (quarterly or half yearly) accounts — these are called interim dividends. Those to be paid at the end of the year are the final or proposed dividends.

Transfers to Reserves

These are amounts that are set aside from the year's profits and will not be available for distribution to shareholders. A typical example of a "reserve" is a capital expenditure reserve. Here, profits made are set aside so that future major repairs can be planned and funded without suddenly needing extra finance.

Retained Profits

These are what is left after the above items have been taken from net profits. On the appropriation account the retained profit for the year is shown separately and added to any retained profits brought forward from previous years. This then gives a figure for retained profits which is carried forward to the next year.

Figure 9 — J Smith Limited
Trading and Profit and Loss Account (Year End 31-12-X7)

		£000s	*£000s*
Trading account	Sales		*200*
	Cost of sales		
	Add opening stock	100	
	Add purchases	150	
		250	
	Less closing stock	150	100
	Gross profit		100
Profit and loss account	Less expenses		50
	Net profit before tax		50
Appropriation account	Less corporation tax		10
	Net profit after tax		40
	Dividends paid and proposed		10
			30
	Transfer to reserves		20
	Retained profits for the year		10
	Add profit and loss account balance brought forward		25
	Profit and loss account balance carried forward to next year		35

This is a typical example of a profit and loss account produced for internal purposes. In practice, the expenses are shown in much more detail. When a profit and loss account is to be produced for external reporting, the format followed is laid down by the **Companies Act 1985** (as amended by the **Companies Act 1989**). There is a choice of four profit and loss account formats and the layout used depends on which one is appropriate (or preferred) for the type of business. Although a detailed analysis of the published profit and loss account formats is beyond the scope of this text, the main headings used are similar to those in the internal profit and loss account. Both the internal and external profit and loss account contain essentially the same information in relation to income, expenses and profit or loss.

THE BALANCE SHEET

WHAT IS A BALANCE SHEET?

The other main financial statement produced from the trial balance is the balance sheet (B/S). The balance sheet shows the wealth or net worth of the business at a particular point in time. The idea is that the difference between the balance sheet at the start of the time period and the balance sheet at the end of the period, is the income generated (adjusted for funds put in by the owners, eg new shares issued, or dividends paid). If a profit and loss account is prepared for the year to 30/11/19X7, then the corresponding balance sheet will be as at 30/11/19X7. The balance sheet can be seen as a "snapshot" of the financial position of the business at a given moment, whereas the profit and loss account shows what has happened over a length of time.

Items are shown on the balance sheet that are capable of being measured in monetary terms, for example the benefits of a good relationship between workers and management would not appear. This is known as the "monetary measurement concept". Another accounting principle used in relation to the balance sheet is that of historic cost. Here, items on the balance sheet are shown at their actual cost, rather than any opinion of their value.

The balance sheet contains details of assets, liabilities and capital and is basically a list of the assets and liabilities at a given point in time (this is usually the last day of the period for which the profit and loss account is prepared).

In simple terms, assets are what the business owns, liabilities are what it owes, and capital is funds that have been put into it by the owner(s). For example, suppose that an individual, "Miss Jones", has £20,000 with which to set up a business. She spends it all on equipment — so at this moment in time her business owns equipment worth £20,000, ie the business has £20,000 of assets. At the same time, the business owes her the £20,000 which she put into it. This is called capital, so as well as having £20,000 worth of assets, the business also has had capital introduced of £20,000. Miss Jones then takes out a £5000 bank overdraft which will be used to pay setting up costs over the next few weeks. The position now is that the business owes the bank £5000 — a liability, but there is also £5000 in the bank (another asset). The financial position of the business can be summarised as follows.

			£
+	**Asset**	Equipment	20,000
+	**Asset**	Cash at bank	5,000
-	**Liability**	Bank overdraft	5,000
=	**Capital**	Capital employed	20,000

This can be expressed as an equation.

$$Assets - liabilities \ = \ capital$$
$$(£20,000 + £5000 - £5000) \ = \ (£20,000)$$
$$(equipment + cash\ at\ bank - bank\ overdraft) \ = \ (capital)$$

This shows the value of the assets of the business in monetary terms (£25,000), ie the balance sheet can be seen as a measure of what the business is worth.

Another way of looking at it is to think of capital and liabilities as sources of finance. Where has the finance come from? Is it capital (funds introduced by the owner or is it liabilities (what the business owes)? Assets can then be considered in terms of how the finance has been used ie what the business owns as a result of using the finance raised. In these terms, the balance sheet can be viewed as an indicator of what funds the business has raised and how these funds have been put to use. It must be remembered that the balance sheet only gives such a picture for any one moment. This is in complete contrast to the profit and loss which measures performance over a period of time.

SOLE TRADERS AND THE BALANCE SHEET

Assets, liabilities and capital are general headings on the balance sheet. There are several sub-headings which are:
- fixed assets
- current assets
- current liabilities
- long-term liabilities
- capital employed which includes adjustments for drawings, capital introduced, and net profit or loss.

Fixed Assets

These are assets (things owned by the business) that have been bought to be used in the business and are not for resale. The most common categories of fixed assets are land and buildings, motor vehicles, fixtures and fittings, and plant, equipment and machinery. These assets tend to have a minimum useful life of at least a year. They initially appear on the balance sheet at the amount they cost to buy. Items like motor vehicles, however, do not hold their value indefinitely. The balance sheet is, among other things, a measure of the value of the business. If, however, all fixed assets were shown on the balance sheet at what they cost to buy, regardless of their age and condition, this would not be a fair reflection of what they are worth. As a way round this, the value of certain fixed assets is reduced on the balance sheet by taking off an amount for wear and tear. This amount is known as *depreciation*.

There are different recognised methods of calculating depreciation, but the general idea is to spread the cost of the asset over its useful life. If a van has been bought for £1000 and is expected to last for four years, one method of depreciating it is to take off £250 each year. In the first year, the value of the van on the balance sheet would be £750, in the second year it would be £500 and so on. All fixed assets are shown on the balance sheet at their cost less any depreciation — this is known as their net book value (nbv). Not all fixed assets are depreciated — land and buildings usually appreciate in value rather than depreciate, so the nbv of property is often the same as the cost. Depreciation reduces the value of fixed assets on the balance sheet but it also affects the profit and loss account where it is shown as an expense. In the example above, the van has a nbv of £750 shown on the balance sheet at the end of the year. In the profit and loss account for the year, £250 will be shown as an expense. It should be noted that charging depreciation in the profit and loss account does not involve any cash movement. The idea of depreciation is the accountants solution to allowing for wear and tear on assets and is just a paper entry.

Current Assets

These are assets that tend to change frequently. The main categories of current assets are stocks, debtors, prepayments and cash balances.

Stocks can include stocks of raw materials, work-in-progress (eg half-finished goods) and stocks of finished goods — these are typical items for a manufacturing business. A retail business will have stock made up of goods that have been bought for resale.

Debtors owe the business money, so they can be customers who have bought goods on credit or they may be employees who have been given a loan by the business. Usually, however, the main debtors are customers — trade debtors.

Prepayments represent deferred expenditure, ie they have been taken out of the profit and loss account as they do not match the accounting period and appear instead on the balance sheet as assets. Prepayments are payments made in advance in respect of costs that have not yet been incurred. A typical example is prepaid insurance.

Cash balances are simply any cash that is physically held, plus any cash in the bank.

Current Liabilities

These are amounts that are owed by the business and expected to be paid back in the short term (usually one year). The main types are trade creditors, accrued expenses (accruals), taxation creditors and bank overdrafts. Any other short-term loans that have to be repaid in the next accounting period, eg hire-purchase agreements, will also be included under current liabilities.

Trade creditors are the suppliers to the business from whom goods have been bought on credit.

Accruals are the opposite of the prepayments noted above. Accrued amounts included under current liabilities represent costs incurred for items consumed, but not paid for, during the period.

For sole traders and partnerships, taxation creditors are the Inland Revenue and HM Customs & Excise. Tax owed to the Inland Revenue will be in relation to employee deductions — any personal income tax owed does not appear on a sole trader or partnership balance sheet. If the business is registered for VAT, any VAT due up to the end of the period is included under current liabilities. If a VAT refund is due, it will come under current assets.

Although bank overdrafts often continue for several years, they are classed as current liabilities — they are usually repayable on demand if the bank so wishes.

Long-term Liabilities

These are amounts owed by the business that are due to be paid back after one year. Long-term loans, such as a business development loan to be repaid over five years, come under this heading.

Capital Employed

This shows the amount invested in the business by the owner. On a sole trader's balance sheet, it is shown as follows.

	£
Capital account brought forward	2000
Add capital introduced	3000
Add net profit for the year	4000
	9000
Less drawings	3500
Capital account carried forward	5500

The first line is the previous period's closing capital. After this, any funds put into the business by the owner are added — called "capital introduced".

Under this, the net profit for the period is added. If a net loss has been made, it is subtracted from the figures. These three figures are subtotalled and the drawings are subtracted. "Drawings" is the name given to any personal costs taken from the business — any such costs must not appear in the profit and loss account or the balance sheet. Cash to live on taken from cash sales or from the business bank account is classed as drawings. Other examples are household bills, payments for meals out, clothes, records, etc. The final total is the closing capital for the period — this should be exactly equal to total assets minus total liabilities.

A typical balance sheet for a sole trader is as follows.

Figure 10 — A Trader Limited
Balance Sheet (As at 30-6-19X7)

	£000s	£000s
Fixed assets		
Land and buildings (nbv)		20
Motor vehicles (nbv)		12
Equipment and fixtures (nbv)		11
		43
Current assets		
Trade debtors	15	
Stock	10	
Prepayments	2	
	27	
Current liabilities		
Trade creditors	12	
Accruals	1	
VAT	2	
Bank overdraft	8	
	23	
Net current assets	4	4
Total assets *less current liabilities*		47
Less *long-term liabilities*		14
		33

Continued overleaf

Represented by:		
Capital account brought forward		18
Capital introduced		7
Net profit for the year		$\underline{25}$
		50
Drawings		$\underline{17}$
		$\underline{\underline{33}}$

(nbv = net book value)

Note: sometimes long-term liabilities are shown in the capital account section (the bottom half) of the balance sheet.

LIMITED COMPANIES AND THE BALANCE SHEET

As with the profit and loss account, limited companies prepare a balance sheet for "internal" purposes (basically for use by the management), but are also obliged to produce an external balance sheet for publication. The external balance sheet has to follow one of two formats laid out in the **Companies Act 1985** (as amended by the **Companies Act 1989**). The information contained in the external balance sheet is basically the same as in the internal balance sheet. In addition, the most commonly used external format is very similar to the internal format which is shown as follows.

The top half (assets and liabilities) of an internal company balance sheet is essentially the same as that of the sole trader. Some additional headings are as follows.

Investments

These are shares held in other companies and are shown under fixed assets.

Intangible Assets

These are also a category of fixed assets and are non-physical assets, eg copyright, patents and goodwill. It should be noted that the value of intangible assets such as goodwill cannot be created and can only appear in the balance sheet if there has been an associated cost, for example if another business has been purchased for a sum in excess of its net asset value. There is no reason why certain intangibles cannot appear on a sole trader balance sheet. Goodwill often does but generally they are associated more with the company balance sheet.

Taxation Creditors

Companies pay corporation tax and any tax due appears as a current liability, in addition to the usual PAYE (employee deductions) and VAT amounts due.

Proposed Dividends

Limited companies are owned by their shareholders. The shareholders receive dividends if enough profits have been made. If a dividend has been declared, but not yet paid as at the balance sheet date, it becomes a liability of the company and is shown under current liabilities.

Debentures

This is a type of long-term loan usually secured on the company assets and is listed under long-term liabilities.

Where the company balance sheet is significantly different from the sole trader is the capital employed section. On a company balance sheet the following terms are used:
- issued (or called up) share capital
- share premium account
- other reserves.

Issued Share Capital

This represents the amounts received from shares actually issued and taken up. It is always shown as £1 for every share issued — £1 being the nominal value of each share. If 100,000 shares have been issued for £1 and all the cash received, the issued share capital of the company is £100,000. If, however, there are to be two payments of 50p each and only the first payment has been received, the issued share capital is (50p x 100,000) £50,000. The authorised share capital is the number and type of shares the company is allowed to issue in total. It is often shown on the balance sheet but is for information only and does not form part of the balance sheet.

The Share Premium Account

This holds any amounts received on shares over £1. If 100,000 shares are issued for £1.50, the nominal value of the shares goes into the issued share capital account — this will be £100,000. The balance (£50,000) goes into the share premium account. By law, the share premium account can only be used for a very limited number of purposes. It specifically cannot be used to pay dividends to shareholders.

Other Reserves

These may be capital or revenue reserves. A typical capital reserve arises when property is revalued at above cost. A revenue reserve might be a general reserve. The profit and loss account (or retained earnings) is another revenue reserve.

If the balance sheet for "A Trader" is adjusted to become a typical internal company balance sheet, it appears as follows.

Figure 11 — A Trader Limited
Internal Balance Sheet (As at 30-6-19X7)

	£000s	£000s
Fixed assets		
Intangible assets		100
Goodwill (nbv)		100
Tangible assets		
Land and buildings (nbv)	50	
Plant and machinery (nbv)	120	
Motor vehicles (nbv)	35	
	205	205
Investments		
Shares in group companies		25
		330

Continued overleaf

Current assets		
Trade debtors	125	
Stock	75	
Other debtors	50	
	250	
Creditors		
Amounts falling due within one year		
Trade creditors	105	
Other creditors	80	
Bank overdraft	50	
	235	
Net current assets	15	15
Total assets less current liabilities		345
Creditors — Amounts falling due after one year		
5% Debentures		10
		335
Financed by:		
Share capital		
Authorised:		
Ordinary shares 500,000 at £1 each (£500,000)		
6% Preference shares 100,000 at £1 each (£100,000)		
Issued and fully paid:		
Ordinary shares 150,000 at £1 each	150	
6% Preference shares 50,000 at £1 each	50	
	200	200
Reserves		
Share premium account	50	
General reserve	10	
Profit and loss account	75	
	135	135
		335

Note: companies issue ordinary and preference shares. It is usually the ordinary shares that carry voting rights, while preference shares receive a fixed percentage dividend in priority to ordinary shares.

INTERPRETING ACCOUNTS

WHY INTERPRET ACCOUNTS?

Financial statements like the balance sheet and the profit and loss account, attempt to measure the financial performance of a business, eg "what profit has been made?" or "what assets and liabilities it has?". However, such statements on their own do not answer questions such as:

- has enough profit been made?
- is the business solvent?
- how is the business doing compared to previous years?
- are there any particular problem areas?

One way of shedding some light on these questions is to interpret the financial statements using "accounting ratios". There is no one definitive set of ratios, although there are some that are more commonly used than others. When using ratios the following points should be remembered.

1. The figures thrown up by the ratios are only as accurate as the accounts they have been based on. If, for example, the sales figure contains a significant error, any ratios using the sales figure will be similarly distorted.

2. Applying accounting principles inconsistently or switching to alternative ones can make ratios meaningless. For ratios to be meaningful, like has to be compared with like.

3. Rather than being used in isolation, a more effective way is to use ratios in conjunction with other information available, eg management structure, product ranges, any available industry yardsticks, etc.

4. When making comparisons with other similar businesses, many factors need to considered. Are they of similar size? Do they have the same product range and production and stock valuation methods? Do they have the same types and values of assets, etc?

5. Ratios are far more useful when compared to previous periods — computing a set of ratios just for one period will not be of much use. For example, a change in the gross profit margin from 33% in a previous period to, for example, 28% in the current period is much more

revealing than the absolute value, and should lead management to explore the reasons for this.

6. Different categories are sometimes used for the same ratios, eg someone may use "net profit before tax", while someone else uses "net profit before tax and interest" when computing the same ratio.

Despite the limitations of accounting ratios, they are nonetheless a commonly used analytical tool and can provide valuable insights into the state of the business. Ratios can be classed into the following:

- profitability
- liquidity
- asset usage
- capital structure
- investment.

Many ratios are equally applicable to sole traders, partnerships and limited companies, although there are some that are really only relevant to limited companies. However, it should be remebered when comparing ratios for a limited company with those of a sole trader or partnership that in the case of the former the salaries of directors or working shareholders will be deducted before a net profit figure is struck, whereas the drawings of a sole trader or partner are only deducted after the net profit has been calculated.

Some common profitability ratios are gross profit, net profit and return on capital employed.

The Gross Profit Margin

Gross profit is the average mark-up or margin made on the goods being sold by the business. It is expressed as:

$$\frac{\text{gross profit}}{\text{sales}} \times 100$$

Example

Using the profit and loss account for "J Smith Limited" (as shown in *The Profit and Loss Account* earlier), the gross profit margin is 50%

$$\frac{1000,000}{200,000} \times 100$$

Suppose the previous year's figures had been the following.

Year to 31-12-19X6	*Sales*	£250,000
Year to 31-12-19X6	*Gross profit*	£100,000

This gives a gross profit margin of 40% ($£ \frac{100,000}{250,000} \times 100$).

On the face of it, the sales figure is higher with the same amount actual of gross profit, but when the margin is calculated it is smaller. So for 19X7 the drop in sales is not quite as disastrous as it may first seem. The next step would be to find out why this has happened. One possible reason could be that selling prices have increased or the cost of the goods sold has fallen.

Net Profit

Net profit ratios compare sales to net profit and can show what is happening to overhead expenses:

$$\frac{\text{net profit before tax}}{\text{sales}} \times 100$$

Example

Again using J Smith Limited, the net profit ratio is 25% ($£ \frac{50,000}{200,000} \times 100$), ie for every £100 of sales, £25 net profit has been made. In practice, this would be compared to previous years and any significant changes investigated.

Return on Capital Employed

Return on capital employed (ROCE) is a measure of the profit made in relation to the funds invested in the business. Apart from non-profit making organisations, businesses exist to make profits. They generally do this by getting finance which is then used to generate profits. ROCE can be calculated as:

$$\frac{\text{net profit before interest and tax}}{\text{capital employed}} \times 100$$

Here, any loan or bank interest is added back to the net profit — the logic being that loans and overdrafts are sources of finance and should be excluded. Capital employed is usually taken to be:

$$\text{capital} + \text{reserves} + \text{long-term debts}$$

Example

Using the balance sheet of "A Company Limited" (as shown in *The Balance Sheet* earlier), the capital employed is:

£000s

200 (capital) + 135 (reserves) + 10 (long-term debts – 5% debentures) = 345

If the net profit before tax and interest is £75,000, the ROCE is 21.7% ($\frac{75,000}{345,000}$ × 100). This can then be compared to previous years and to other similar businesses (higher figures of course mean better returns).

Liquidity Ratios

Liquidity ratios can indicate the solvency of a business, ie its ability to pay its debts as they fall due. Two commonly used ratios are the "current ratio" and the "quick (or acid test) ratio".

The current ratio is simply the ratio of current assets to current liabilities and is calculated as follows:

$$\frac{\text{current assets}}{\text{current liabilities}}$$

Example

Again using the balance sheet of "A Company Limited", the current ratio is 1.06 (£ $\frac{250,000}{235,000}$). This means that the current liabilities are only just covered by current assets. This may be above, below or just average for the business and the industry — this is another ratio that really needs to be compared to other years and similar businesses for it to be of use. A negative ratio, however (when current liabilities are more than current assets), is usually a cause for concern, especially if it persists for more than one accounting period.

The current ratio is also sometimes known as the "working capital ratio". Working capital is the difference between current assets and current liabilities. It is important to businesses as it finances day-to-day activities so long as there is a good circulation of it, ie enough stock has to be sold and debts collected for the suppliers to be paid.

The quick (acid test) ratio is a more sensitive test as it excludes stocks (stocks are generally slower at being converted into cash than debtors). It can be expressed as follows:

$$\frac{\text{current assets less stock}}{\text{current liabilities}}$$

For "A Company Limited", this ratio is 0.74 ($£ \frac{250,000-75,000}{235,000}$). A quick ratio of around 1 is generally considered acceptable but as with other ratios it needs to be compared to previous years and other like businesses.

Asset Usage Ratios

Asset usage ratios provide an indication of how well the business is managing its assets. Two typical ratios are "average debt collection period" and "rate of stock turnover".

The average debt collection period measures how long debtors, on average, take to pay. It is worked out as follows and is expressed in number of days:

$$\frac{\text{average debtors}}{\text{sales}} \times 365$$

The figure for average debtors is taken as the trade debtors on this year's balance sheet plus trade debtors from the previous year's balance sheet, divided by two. The trade debtors on the 19X7 balance sheet for "A Company Limited" are £125,000. If last year's figure was £105,000, the average debtors are £115,000 (£125,000 +£$\frac{105,000}{2}$).

If sales are £550,000 for this year, then the average collection period is 76 days ($£ \frac{115,000}{550,000} \times 365$). This can then be compared to other years to see whether the business's credit control has improved.

The rate of stock turnover is particularly useful in a business such as a retail shop where goods are brought for stock and subsequently sold and shows the number of times the average stock held is sold in the period. Average stock is the previous year's balance sheet stock figure plus this year's figure, divided by two. If "A Company Limited" had stocks of £45,000 on the previous year's balance sheet, the average stock is £60,000 (£75,000 + £$\frac{45,000}{2}$). The rate of stock turnover is calculated as follows:

$$\frac{\text{sales}}{\text{average stock}}$$

If sales are £550,000 for 19X7, the rate of stock turnover is 9.17 times ($£ \frac{550,000}{60,000}$). As ever this needs to be compared to other years in order to see the trend. The higher the rate, the less time stock is sitting on the shelves as tied up working capital. The stock turnover ratio is more meaningful if the profit margin is taken out of the calculaton. Thus the stocks should either be valued at their re-sale price or the cost of sales figures should replace sales. In both cases the VAT should again be stripped out. The resulting number will show how many times a year the stock is turned over (eg eight times) and hence the average time the goods are held in stock (6½ weeks in this case). This can be compared with the lead time for re-supply and/or the length of credit offered by suppliers.

Capital Structure Ratios

Capital structure (or gearing) ratios try to say something about the long-term financing policy between equity (ordinary shares plus reserves) and other forms of long-term finance, eg preference shares, long-term loans and debentures. There are too many gearing ratios to discuss each one individually but a typical one is the debt to equity ratio. This is calculated as:

$$\frac{debt}{equity} \times 100$$

Example

Debt is any long-term debt. Looking at "A Company Limited", its only long-term debt is the 5% debentures. Its equity consists of the following.

Issued ordinary share capital	£150,000
Reserves	£135,000
	£285,000

This gives a debt/equity ratio of 3.5% (£ $\frac{10,000}{285,000}$ × 100), which is low. A low-geared company has raised finance mainly through issuing ordinary shares, while a high-geared company has a bigger proportion of long-term debts. In times of recession, it is often the highly geared companies that struggle more since the loan/interest payments have to be kept whereas in a low-geared company, dividends are only paid to ordinary shareholders if there are enough profits.

Investment Ratios

Investment ratios can give ordinary shareholders information on how the company has done in relation to its ordinary shares. There are many such ratios (again too many to discuss each one in detail) but a typical ratio is return on equity:

$$\frac{\text{net profit after tax less preference dividend}}{\text{equity}} \times 100$$

Example

Equity is the issued share capital plus reserves. For "A Company Limited", if it is net profit after tax for 19X7 is £50,000, this ratio is 17.54% ($\frac{50,000}{285,000} \times$ 100). It shows what is left for ordinary shareholders after all other business costs have been met. This can also usefully be expressed as net earnings per share and can be used by shareholders to evaluate the success or otherwise of their investment. As with other ratios, it really needs to be viewed in relation to past years or similar businesses to be of use.

Another useful management ratio is calculation of the break-even point. This is the volume of sales which at the current gross margin produces just enough gross profit to cover the firm's total overheads (and, in the case of a sole trader or partnership, enough drawings to enable them to sustain an adequate income). This is calculated by dividing the total overheads by the gross margin percentage (ie if the overheads were £50,000 and the gross margin 25% the break-even sales figure would be £50,000 ÷ 0.25 = £200,000). This can be divided by actual annual sales (eg £300,000) and the result (66%) used as a measure of the firms resilience. The lower the percentage, the safer the business is should things go wrong. The break-even can also be expressed in terms of the calendar and in this case the firm has to trade from 1 January to 31 August to cover the overheads and earn its profit in the rest of the year. Alternatively, if it is trading six days a week, it covers its overheads Monday through Thursday and earns profits on Friday and Saturday.

LEGAL IMPLICATIONS OF INCORPORATION

WHAT IS INCORPORATION?

If a business incorporates itself, it becomes a limited company. There are three main types of limited company:
- a private company limited by shares
- a private company limited by guarantee
- a public company.

In a private company limited by shares, the shareholder's liability is restricted to the amount of any unpaid shares they hold. This is the most common type of company as far as small businesses are concerned.

In a private company limited by guarantee, the shareholder's liability is restricted to the amount they have agreed to pay in the event of the company being wound up. This is a more unusual type of company and typically one such as a sports club or charity, where earning a profit is not the primary motive.

In a public company, the shareholder's liability is the same as for a private company limited by shares. A public company (plc) must have an authorised share capital of at least £50,000 at the time of incorporation. It must also have issued and paid up share capital to at least one quarter of the nominal value of each share together with the whole of any premium. The main advantage of being a plc is that it can raise finance by offering its shares for sale to the public.

Generally, the two main consequences of becoming incorporated are the limited liability of members (shareholders) and the company being a legal entity in its own right.

Private companies must have at least one director and a company secretary, whereas plcs need to have at least two directors and a secretary.

LEGAL REQUIREMENTS

In relation to a company's accounts, it must:

- keep accounting records
- send its accounts to the Register of Companies.

A set of accounts is normally sent every year to the Registrar (private companies have 10 months from the end of the accounting period to submit their accounts plcs have 7 months). The accounts sent to the Registrar are known as the "published accounts". If the accounts are submitted late, the company incurs late filing penalties in the form of fines.

CONTENT OF ACCOUNTS

The accounts delivered to the Registrar include:
- a profit and loss account (or income and expenditure account if it is a non-profit making body)
- a balance sheet signed by a director
- a signed audit report (all except certain small companies have to have their accounts audited [independently examined] by a registered auditor)
- a signed director's report (or signed by the secretary)
- notes to the accounts
- group accounts if applicable.

EXEMPTIONS

If a company is classed as small or medium sized there are certain exemptions available in relation to what is filed with the registrar. Small and medium-sized companies in this context are defined by the **Companies Act 1985** (as amended by the **Companies Act 1989**). A small company must meet two of the following conditions:
- the annual turnover is £2.8 million or less
- the total of its fixed and current assets is £1.4 million or less
- the average number of employees is 50 or less.

If at least two of these are met then the company need only send to the Registrar:
- a shortened form of balance sheet and notes
- a special auditors report if required.

A medium-sized company must satisfy two of the following:

- the annual turnover is £11.2 million or less
- the total of its fixed and current assets is £5.6 million or less
- the average number of employees is 250 or less.

A medium-sized company can send the following to the Registrar:

- a full balance sheet
- a shortened form of profit and loss account
- special auditors report
- directors report
- notes to the accounts.

These are external reporting exemptions only. Small and medium-sized companies will still produce a full set of accounts for internal reporting purposes, eg for use by management or the shareholders.

Published accounts will also usually include a cash flow statement which shows the movement of cash during an accounting period.

CHAPTER TWO

COST AND MANAGEMENT ACCOUNTING

In today's business environment manager's are expected to be able to interpret, monitor and control performance within their departments and be able to make an overall contribution to future financial plans within their company.

The financial situation of an organisation is normally expressed in its company accounts but company accounts are, on the whole, produced for the benefit of investors and contain financial information highlighting the financial strengths and weaknesses of the organisation in relation to its assets and liabilities. These accounts are necessary by law but are insufficient and sometimes irrelevant for internal purposes when considering pricing, budgeting, planning and controlling internal costs.

Cost and management accounting is a collection of simple common sense rules and procedures designed to be of practical help to managers. It makes management aware of how well the company is performing against specific objectives by identifying, presenting and interpreting information within a framework which assists management in formulating strategy, controlling activities, decision making, optimising the use of resources and safeguarding assets.

THE CORPORATE PLAN

In any major organisation or company, the Directors are likely to have produced a detailed plan of how they see the company developing. This plan is usually called the corporate plan and once it has been agreed by the board of directors it becomes the blueprint of what the directors expect the company to achieve over a given period of time in the future.

In effect it is the vision for the future and gives rise to the mission statement and ultimately the objectives or key result areas (KRAs) set for every section and department throughout the company.

The directors and senior management produce a statement outlining the company's objectives for the forthcoming budget period. They also prepare a forecast of the general economic conditions within the industry and the company. Then each department produces a mini-plan based on this statement and forecast which are incorporated into the appropriate budgets. These budgets are then assimilated into the corporate plan for approval by the directors and once it has been agreed it becomes the blueprint of what the directors expect the company to achieve over a given future period of time.

The corporate plan contains very detailed parameters for the coming trading year. It is also likely to have been "projected" to provide an outline of the company's progress for the next five (or sometimes up to 10) years. Separate figures are shown for each year, and although they cannot be accurate, the idea is to show the trend the company is likely to follow during that period.

THE BASICS OF COSTING

Cost is a word used to describe the money spent on a particular item. In a business context it is possible to talk about the cost of labour or the cost of running a department or the cost of a particular product or service sold to customers.

Every business organisation incurs costs no matter what that business is. Costs are incurred on the resources consumed by the organisation when carrying out its business objective of satisfying customer needs. The resources that are consumed are materials, people effort, bought in services, the use of equipment, and even money itself, which incurs an interest cost.

Costing is the analysis of costs so that they can be allocated to products/services, activities, departments, and specific time periods. This objective analysis of costs is typified when they are charged to the end product or department consuming such costs.

Costs are related to some appropriate object, function, or service, eg a car, a loaf, a medical operation, etc are cost units. Some managers may have the responsibility for a profit centre which is part of a business accountable for costs and revenues. (A profit centre may also be called a business centre, business unit or strategic business unit.)

Coding

A cost accounting system normally involves a great deal of documentation and in order to make sure that costs are charged correctly through the cost centres it is necessary for the organisation to adopt a formal coding system.

Example

A large bakery may have the following.

Divisions	bread 01; confectionery 02; biscuit 03; wholesale 04; retail 05.
Factories	Manchester 001; Birmingham 002; London 003; Bristol 004; Glasgow 005.
Cost Centre	maintenance 001; production 002; distribution 003; R&D 004; sales 005.
Expense	in this example a four figure digit: 0000

So the expense of raw materials (code 1234) in the production of bread for the Manchester factory would be coded as 01/001/002/1234.

The necessity for a company to inform and train personnel in the recognition and use of a costing system is paramount for the system to work effectively.

COSTING SYSTEMS

It is up to the organisation to choose the costing method that is suitable for the type of goods produced or the services offered. There are two major methods of cost accounting systems:

- absorption costing
- marginal costing.

The difference in the two methods is the way the method deals with the treatment of fixed production overheads.

Any product cost system should determine the cost of the finished product built up from its cost elements. The cost elements are the constituent parts of costs according to the factors upon which expenditure is incurred, namely about, materials and expenses.

Figure 12 — Unit Cost Structure: The Elements of a Cost Based on Absorption Costing

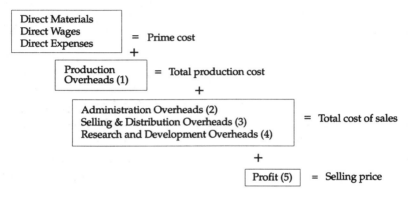

Notes

1. Production overheads are sometimes known as factory overheads and by adding the prime cost a total factory cost will have been identified. Production overheads include indirect production costs and possibly some factory costs associated with production.
2. Administrative overheads will include the non factory costs of operating the company.
3. Selling and distribution costs are those which include the cost of promoting the company's products or service and distributing to the consumer.
4. Research are costs incurred in working on new products or services. Development work is normally associated with costs incurred on existing products, processes or services.
5. A profit loading is sometimes added to the total cost of sales to arrive at a unit selling price.

Direct costs which make up the prime cost can be allocated to the cost unit because they can easily be identified with it.

Labour

In some industries labour costs may form more than half of the total running costs of an organisation. Manufacturing industries used to be very labour intensive with control of direct labour costs justifiably getting a high profile. With the coming of automation and robotics this is no longer the case, resulting in attention shifting to machine costs, material costs and indirect labour costs. Nevertheless, labour costs are still significant in many organisations and need to be carefully costed.

Direct labour or wages are those paid to people directly concerned in producing a product or providing a service. Examples of this include operatives, assemblers, receptionist, etc. The wages that support a service or organise production are called indirect labour. Examples of indirect labour are foremen, maintenance personnel, quality inspectors, cleaning staff, etc. Indirect labour is treated as an overhead.

Direct wages are calculated on the basis or either time or output. In time based systems the wage of a worker is calculated by recording the number of hours worked by the basic rate per hour, eg 37 hrs per week × £4.00 per hour = £148.00 per week. If the employee works over the basic hours for the shift, day or week the payment is made up of overtime (this is charged to overheads — see *Overheads* later in this chapter), which can be calculated on a basic rate × 0.5 or any other agreed formula. Time-related payment systems will frequently include bonuses and other payments, eg shift premiums, safety allowances, good timekeeping.

In some organisations it is possible to give the worker a degree of control over the amount of money they earn and the employer an increased output. This type of system is called an incentive scheme. The two common schemes associated with output based payments are piecework and bonus schemes.

Piecework is paid on the basis of an agreed rate per unit or operation, for the number of units produced or operation carried out. An example of this is when a machinist is paid at a rate of £3.10 per 100 units. He or she makes 8230 units during the week of which through an independent inspection process 130 are rejected. On piecework the machinist is only paid for good production so this machinist will be paid 8100 × £3.10 (per 100) = £251.10. The example given is one of straight piecework but it is possible to have the rate progressively increased at various output levels. This is known as differential piecework.

With bonus systems there is usually the combination of a flat rate per hour with a bonus for achieving a given output. The bonus is calculated (in the majority of cases) between the savings made between the actual time taken and the agreed target time for the job. To calculate wages documentation is needed, which usually takes the form of timecards or timesheets. These documents are used by accounting staff to prepare the payroll and to charge labour costs to appropriate cost units and cost centres. Direct labour, including any bonuses and premium rates, can be directly charged to the products/services worked on. Indirect labour, an example being overtime which is charged to overheads is first channelled to cost centres and then absorbed into product/service costs by using overhead recovery rates.

Materials

Organisations may hold stocks of materials or components in their stores for issue at a later date. The purchase and subsequent issue of these materials is also documented at various stages to ensure that volume and values are known and are charged to the right cost units and cost centres. If materials are ordered for a specific purpose, the invoice can be specifically charged to the cost unit and cost centre concerned.

Material costs are some times difficult to identify because purchase prices of raw materials and goods bought for re-sale vary over time. This problem can be solved by using various options to price stores issue.

1. *First in first out (FIFO).* This method issues stock first at old prices. Remaining stock is therefore valued at recent prices for balance sheet purposes.

2. *Last in first out (LIFO).* More popular in the USA but not accepted as a valid basis by the Inland Revenue in the UK.

3. *Standard price.* All similar materials are held in store at the one predetermined standard price specified and are issued at that value.

4. *Weighted average price.* This is a compromise between FIFO and LIFO values, materials are issued at the same average price.

Once the materials have been valued, direct materials can be charged out to the cost units by using a relevant job number. Indirect materials, ie those materials which do not appear in the final product are charged to the cost centre incurring them, to be charged to cost units later as part of the total overhead recovery.

Expenses

Direct expenses can be charged directly to the job concerned. The invoice for the expenses can be charged to the cost unit in much the same way as direct labour and direct materials are charged to the relevant job number. Indirect expenses have to be charged to the cost centres along with indirect labour and indirect materials. All these three indirect costs will be treated on an overhead recovery basis.

To summarise, direct labour and direct expenses are those costs which can be directly identified with the product or job or service. To ascertain the full cost of the cost unit it is necessary to include the indirect costs, ie the overheads.

Overheads

Any cost which cannot be identified with a specific product or service is an "indirect cost". Indirect costs, or overheads, have to be apportioned and then broken down further by a process known as absorption. The first step necessary to find out what overheads should be included in the product or service being provided is to divide the organisation into cost centres.

A cost centre can be likened to a "mail box" where overhead expenditure is posted. The cost centre can be a location (eg a production department) or a function (eg quality control) and is given a code so the expenditure incurred is posted through this code number to the appropriate cost centre.

Some of the costs are specific to the cost centre, eg where a maintenance facility exists for the sole use of the machine shop, this cost could be described as a cost centre direct cost. Others are of a general nature, eg the rent for the whole of the organisation which have to be equitably shared over all the cost centres. This process is called "cost apportionment". An example of this is where a general purpose machine is producing a range of different products it is not possible to determine directly how much rent or insurance should be borne by product A as opposed to product B. This is because overhead costs are not incurred by product.

Apportionment of Overheads

Cost apportionment is the charging of proportions of each indirect or overhead cost item to cost centres using an appropriate basis of apportionment so as to reflect the relative use of that cost item by each cost centre.

Example cost	*Basis of apportionment*
Rent	Area or volume occupied
Insurance of machines	Capital values of machines
Insurance of buildings	Area or volume occupied
Supervision	Number of personnel employed
Depreciation of buildings	Area or volume occupied
Indirect wages	Number of personnel employed
Power	Machine hours, horse power or horse power/hour
Cleaning	Area or volume occupied
Light and heat	Area or volume occupied
Canteen	Number of personnel employed

Cost apportionment should be on a basis which is described as fair, reasonable or equitable.

Example

The total rent of a building is budgeted at £20,000 and its total area is 10,000 square metres. There are within the building three clearly defined departments: A = 5000 square metres: B = 3000 square metres and C = 2000 square metres. The allocation of the rent would be:

$$\frac{\text{Total cost be apportioned} \times \text{each cost centres share of the basis}}{\text{Total apportionment basis}}$$

$$\text{Department A} = \frac{£200,000 \times 5000 \text{ square metres}}{10,000 \text{ square metres}} = £10,000 \text{ square metres}$$

$$\text{Department B} = \frac{£20,000 \times 2000 \text{ square metres}}{10,000 \text{ square metres}} = 4,000 \text{ square metres}$$

$$\text{Department C} = \frac{£20,000 \times 3000 \text{ square metres}}{10,000 \text{ square metres}} = £6000 \text{ square metres}$$

By spreading the overheads of a cost centre over all the products passing through the cost centre it is possible to include all the overhead costs in the total cost of the product or service. The process by which this is equitably done is called overhead absorption or overhead recovery.

The usual way of doing this is to record the amount of time in either machine hours or labour hours that a product is worked on in a cost centre and multiply these hours by an overhead absorption rate (OAR). This will indicate the cost of the overheads which must be included in the cost of the product or service.

The OAR for a cost centre is:

$$\frac{\text{Estimated overheads for cost centre}}{\text{Estimated units of absorption base}} = \text{predetermined OAR for CC}$$

Example

The estimated number of machine hours to be worked in the mixing cost centre for the coming year will be 35,000 hours and the total estimated production overhead costs for this period will be £227,500.

The general production OAR will be £ $\frac{227,500}{35,000}$ = 6.5

An example of the use of the OAR would be if 10 batches of bread are made in the mixing room every hour on the XYZ machine.

Direct costs (materials and labour)	=	860.00
Production overhead cost 1 hour × £6.50	=	6.50
		866.50

This equates to £86.65 per batch.

The OAR base is decided on the basis that it reflects the load on a cost centre. For this reason it is generally assumed that time-based methods (labour and machine hours) are chosen. A base decided upon direct labour hours is normally used where the work is labour intensified. This base uses information based upon the hours previously recorded for wages purposes. An organisation which is highly mechanised uses a machine hour base for its overhead recovery calculations.

In all cases, the OAR is calculated using estimates because the actual overheads cannot be identified until the end of an accounting period. At the end of an accounting period, adjustments are made which take into account the actual overheads and the difference between the estimated figures. The differences are known as under absorption and over absorption. These figures have to be calculated because the profit for the period is based on actual figures.

If the overheads absorbed by production are greater than the actual overheads this is known as over absorption and conversely if under the actual figure it is known as under absorption.

Non-production Overheads

Non-production overheads, such as administration, sales, research development and numerous others have all to be included in the cost of the product or service. There is a difficulty in absorbing these overheads and generally the problem is dealt by either taking a percentage of production cost or a percentage of sales value.

Depreciation

Having dealt with most of the overheads that are included in the costing of a product the remaining overhead, that of depreciation, needs to be addressed. Depreciation is the decline in value, due to wear and the passage of time, of fixed assets. Depreciation costs differ from other overheads in that the amount charged in a period of time is decided by the organisation and that there is no movement in cash. It is important that the cost of expensive assets are costed into the product or service and depreciation is the most practical way to do this. The method of calculating depreciation can be grouped into two categories:

• time

• volume of production.

There are two common methods of calculating depreciation based on a time concept — the "straight line method" and the "reducing balance method". The latter method is usually more acceptable to the Inland Revenue.

Example — straight line method

The straight line method reduces the value of an asset by an equal amount each year. For example, a vehicle purchased at £15,000 is expected to last five years and will have an estimated residual value of £2000 (although some assets are written down to zero value). The amount to be depreciated is therefore £13,000.

Example — reducing balance method

The reducing balance method uses a predetermined percentage to write down the value of the asset in decreasing amounts. The amount of depreciation is charged each year and the percentage chosen will eventually write off the asset over a number of years.

Example — production unit method

A fairer reflection of the depreciation charge within production departments is the production unit method of charging depreciation.

This method is based on the volume of production in a period using a previously calculated depreciation charge.

METHODS OF COSTING

It is important that the method of costing is suitable to the way the services are provided or the goods manufactured. There are two main methods of costing:
- specific order costing
- continuous operation costing.

Specific Order Costing

This is the basic cost accounting method applicable where work consists of separate contracts, jobs or batches. In specific order costing, all the direct costs are charged to the cost unit and overheads are charged to the cost centres and then absorbed according to the time taken. This is necessary because all the jobs and contracts are individual and different from each other so the overheads have to be spread over the orders in an equitable manner.

In specific order costing there are three main sub divisions: job costing, batch costing and contract costing.

Job costing

By creating a job card (each with a given number) it is possible to charge all costs incurred to a particular job.

Figure 13 — Diagram of a Job Card

JOB CARD COST										Job No: 0971			
Customer: B				Customer Order No: 59821									
Job description: NGR Modulators — adjusted										Start date:			
Estimate ref:				Invoice No:						Delivery date:			
Quoted Price:				Invoice Price:						Despatch date:			

Materials						Labour							Overheads			
Date	Req No	Qty	Price	Cost		Date	Cost Ctr	Hrs	Rate	Bonus	Cost		Hrs	OAR	Cost	
				£	p						£	p			£	p
14.7	5823	1	8.45	8	45	14.7	021	7	6.50	–	45	50	7	5	35	00
		2	2.70	5	40	15.7	022	7	4.00	–	28	00	7	5	35	00
		1	80.00	80	00	18.7	035	5	6.00	–	30	00	5	5	25	00
15.7	5973	20	2.70	54	00											
Total C/f				147	85	Total C/f					103	50	Total		95	00

Expenses						Job Cost Summary	Actual		Estimate	
							£	p	£	p
Date	Ref	Description	Cost							
			£	p		Direct Materials B/f	147	85		
17.7		Sub-contractor	50	00		Direct Expenses B/f	50	00		
						Direct Labour B/f	103	50		
						= Prime Cost	301	35		
						Factory Overheads B/f	95	00		
						= Factory Cost	396	35		
						Selling & Admin Overheads	79	27		
						% on Factory Cost				
						= Total Cost	475	62		
						Invoice Price	550	00		
		Total C/f	50	00		Job Profit/Loss	74	38		

Comments

Job card completed by:

The systematic recording of relevant detail to that particular job or service is made, together with a charge of the direct costs incurred and a proportion of the overheads. A job cost summary identifies the actual costs incurred with the estimated costs. The difference between the invoice price and the actual cost of the job/service gives an indication of the profit or loss made. Job costing is ideal for one-off jobs and bespoked provision.

Batch costing

The costing procedure is identical to that of job costing but differs in the fact that it is a form of costing where a quantity of identical products are manufactured in a batch. Each batch is treated as a separate job with the result that all material, labour and other costs that it is economically viable to identify with the batch, will be allocated to it. Overheads will be absorbed into the batch on either a machine hour or direct labour hour basis. On completion of the batch the cost per unit will be calculated by dividing the batch cost by the number of good units produced. Batch costing is used in food manufacture, plastics and rubber industries, and similar industries.

Contract costing

Again, the costing of contracts is similar to that of job costing, but is normally implemented for work which is of a long duration. For example, in the construction industry the main body of work will be carried out on a site. The site is a self-contained unit which will incur costs which are of a direct and indirect (overheads) nature which can be charged directly to the contract, eg supervisory salaries, power, telephones, transport.

Continuous Operation Costing

This is applicable where goods or services result from a sequence of continuous or repetitive operations or processes. Costs are averaged over the units produced during the period.

Service costing

Many organisations provide a service rather than deliver a product, eg a doctor, solicitors, a local authority, hospitals, hotels, etc. There is also the internal services provided within an organisation which need an internal pricing system to provide management with information about comparative costs and efficiency.

To define a cost unit that represents a suitable measure of the service provided is a difficulty in service costing. A composite cost unit is considered to be the most useful.

For example, a hospital may identify the number of operations performed which is an appropriate unit to identify in hospital of patients undergoing a specific operation within a cost centre. Colleges may identify the cost unit on a tariff matrix basis (time managed units for external funding by a national funding body). This is based on the number of full or part-time students taking a specific course.

Process costing

This is a continuous or repetitive operation in manufacturing certain products. Bought in raw materials enter in at process 1 and then value, in the form of labour and overheads, is added to the process. Once the process is completed, the finished product from process 1 becomes the input material to the next process and so on until the product is completed ready for sale.

Losses incurred during the manufacturing process are quite normal in continuous process. Output losses sometimes occur in weight or volume because of some inherent characteristic of the process. These losses are called normal losses and are unavoidable and they are included as part of the cost of good production. Some of the loss may be offset by selling it as waste and this will help reduce total costs.

Figure 14 — Diagram of Process Costing

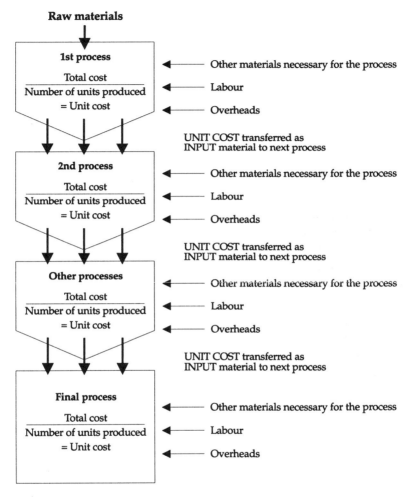

Example

A food manufacturer has a normal wastage of 8% in the initial process of converting raw material into the next processing stage. The cost of this initial process can be reduced by selling the waste for £15.00 per tonne. Input material of 250 tonnes at £60 per tonne. Labour and overheads are £7850. The cost per tonne is as follows.

	Tonnes	£	
Input material	250	15,000	
Labour & overheads		7,850	
		22,850	
Less normal loss	20	300	(income from waste)
Good production	230	22,550	

Cost per tonne of good production = $\frac{22,550}{230}$ = £98.04

There are also losses, and even gains, that occur in the manufacturing process which are above the level expected. These are classed as abnormal process losses or abnormal process gains and are costed at the good production rate.

Considering the data in the previous example, except that the good production is 225 tonnes, the following calculations can be made.

Abnormal loss	=	Actual loss – normal loss
	=	(250 – 225) – (8% of 250)
	=	25 – 20
Abnormal loss	=	5 tonnes

	Tonnes	£	
Input material	250	15,000	
Labour & overheads		7,850	
		22,850	
Less normal loss	20	300	(income from waste)
Less abnormal loss	5 (98.04 × 5)	492	
Good production	225	22, 058	

The five tonnes of abnormal loss can also be sold at the scrap rate for £15 per tonne. The abnormal loss will be £417 (492 – 75) and will be debited to the profit and loss account. Conversely, say there is an abnormal gain of three tonnes the calculations are as follows.

	Tonnes	£	
Input material	250	15,000	
Labour & overheads		7,850	
Abnormal gain	3	294	
	253	23,144	
Less normal loss	20	300	(income from waste)
Good production	233	22,844	

Because the abnormal gain is 3 tonnes of good production there was only 17 tonnes of normal scrap instead of 20 tonnes available for sale. Thus the benefit of £294 from the abnormal gain must be reduced by £45 (3 x £15) which is the amount of scrap sales lost and the profit and loss account credited £249.

Equivalent Units in Process Costing

At the end of each accounting period it is normal to have stock items which are either the raw materials required in a manufacturing process or finished goods ready for sale. There is also the stock which has progressed from the raw material stage and is in various states of completion towards the finished product. This stock is called "work in progress" which still has a cost value because material, labour and a proportion of overheads have been added to it during the manufacturing process.

In process costing this presents the accountant with a number of calculations to perform to gain a correct value of this work in progress for stock valuation purposes. The accountant calculates the amount of work which is in the process of being completed and translates this into equivalent units of finished production. This means that calculations have to be made at the various stages to ascertain how much material, labour and overheads have been used in the process (calculated on a percentage basis) and then translated into equivalent completed units.

Example

A chemical company is processing raw materials and at the end of the process there are 8000 completed units of production, with 500 partly completed to 60% of complete production.

$$
\begin{aligned}
\text{Total equivalent units} \ &= \ 8000 + 60\% \ (500) \\
&= \ 8000 + 300 \\
&= \ 8300
\end{aligned}
$$

The total costs for the period would then be spread over the total completed equivalent units. Sometimes there are estimates that have to made of the work in progress which takes into consideration all the various cost elements. The same principles are adhered to as in the above example but each cost element is treated separately and the individual element costs per unit are added to give the cost of the complete unit.

Example

In a period of production the costs were as follows.

Materials	£ 16,000
Labour	£ 8,500
Overheads	£ 3,500
	£27,000

Production was 4000 completed units and 600 partly complete. The degree of completion of the cost elements of the work in progress was as follows.

Materials	75%
Labour	65%
Overheads	40%

The total equivalent production cost per complete unit and the value of the work in progress is as follows.

Figure 15 — Sample of Total Equivalent Production Cost Per Complete Unit and Work in Progress

Cost elements	Equivalent units in work in progress	+	Completed units	=	Total equivalent production	Total costs	Cost per unit
Materials	600 × 75% = 450	+	4000	=	4450	16,000	3.595
Labour	600 × 65% = 390	+	4000	=	4390	8500	1.936
Overheads	600 × 40% = 240	+	4000	=	4240	3500	0.825
						£28,000	£6.356

Value of completed production = 4000 × £6.356 = £25,424.
Value of work in progress = £28,000 – £25,424 = £2,576.

BUDGETING

If an organisation is to get the best out of a cost and management system it must be provided with information about the future as well as the past. A control method which is familiar to most organisations is budgetary control.

The word budget is readily known to the layperson because households will plan its expenditure (community tax, gas, electricity, holidays, food, transport, etc) on a month to month basis should be and in the light of the income that will be coming into the household. This principle reflects the similarity to a corporate budget where an organisation plans what its expenditure should be against the revenue expected to be generated. This principle is expressed over a given time period.

PREPARING THE BUDGET

There are defined rules and procedures when drawing up the budget and many organisations produce a yearly guide or manual for their management in the preparation of the master and functional budgets. (The master budget is prepared from a number of departmental budgets and comprises a projected balance sheet, a projected profit and loss account and projected cash flow statement.) Once the master budget has been prepared it will be examined to see if what is projected to happen falls within the overall corporate strategy and if it is feasible. During the preparation of the budgeting process it will become apparent that there is a limiting factor or key factor as it is sometimes called that will limit the activities of the organisation. For example, it may be that sales are projecting a large increase but to realise this increase would require considerable extra resources in the production area which in turn would require extra financial commitment by the owners of capital.

Once approval has been given the budget becomes a control document for management when the defined time period has been entered. The control is exercised by management when there are variances between what should happen and what actually happens. These variances, if they are of sufficient importance, will be investigated by management and corrective action formulated to bring results back to the budgeted figure.

SETTING THE BUDGET

There are mainly two ways to set a budget. One way is to take information from the previous year, looking specifically at the appropriate accounting period to clarify any seasonal variations and then adjust these figures in line with inflation, changes in prices, costs and activity levels. This method is called "incremental budgeting".

The other method is to take a clean sheet of paper and start completely afresh. This method is called "zero based budgeting" which promotes fresh and hopefully innovatory thinking. It has the advantage of questioning everything by making the manager justify all resources, expenditure and revenue. Although a time-consuming method, it is worthwhile to examine the budgets on this basis once every three years.

The sales budget will probably be the first budget that is produced because sales volume is normally the limiting factor in most organisations. The sales director and his or her team will look at the existing markets and level of business, together with the anticipation of future developments based on feedback from internal reports, external market forecasts and new product development. A very important input into this process is intelligence regarding competitor activity and not just what the competition is currently doing but rather what can be anticipated over the budget period.

When the sales budget has been approved in a manufacturing organisation the production budget (in non-manufacturing organisations this budget is called an operations budget) will need to equate to the projected sales but will be regulated, to some degree, by projected stock levels and the use of sub-contractors if buying in services or goods. The production budget should specify labour requirements, raw materials, production overheads and machine time consumed. It should project the products to be made, when this should take place and in which department. Departmental overhead budgets are prepared on the basis of the level of service required to allow the sales and production functions to meet their budgets. Similarly, the selling and distribution budgets will be geared to the sales budget and the administration budget to the projected overall level of activity.

There will be ancillary budgets such as manpower budgets, materials purchase, research and development produced by the organisation which will have to be accounted for in the overall expenditure analysis.

All the budgets will finally be incorporated into the master budget which will project the profit and loss account balance sheet together with a major projection of the monthly cash flow requirements in the cash budget. The capital budget will also be a major feature of the budgetary committee and this will be formulated in line with organisational objectives. This budget is a collation of planned expenditure in both the replacement and purchase of new assets which may be a requirement to facilitate achieving the projected budgets.

Figure 16 — Budget Relationships

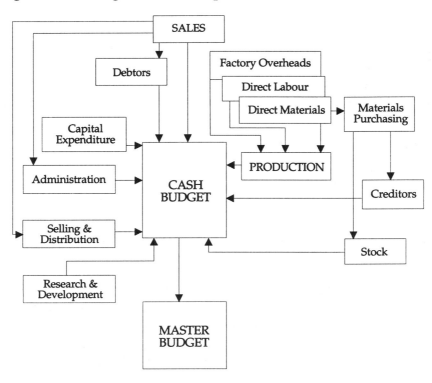

The diagram is only a summary of the main budgets. From the diagram it will be noticed that most of the budgets are interlocked with the cash budget. All budgets will contribute to the master budget.

CONTROLLING THE BUDGET

When the organisation enters the budgeted time period it will produce, on a monthly basis, a budget report which gives a comparison of actual results against budgeted. The manager is given information in the form of a report on the actual costs that have been incurred, and in some cases revenue which has been generated, within their department. From this information a comparison of the two figures can be made and the difference is entered on the report as a variance. If actual costs are below the budgeted figure then the variance is a favourable, but if actual revenue is below the budgeted figure then it is an adverse variance. The report will also highlight the figures on a cumulative basis, ie the total results of expenditure and revenue against budget for the financial year to date (that is including the months previous to the one under review). This will enable the manager to see a more composite picture of the financial state of the organisation and not just the current month's results. (This is quite important because decisions are sometimes made by examining one month's figures instead of looking at the total picture.)

Figure 17 — An Example of a Budget Report

Period .... Department											
Cost Code	Description of Expense	Current Month				Cumulative				Last Year			
		Budgeted	Actual	Variance (£)	%	Budgeted	Actual	Variance (£)	%	Budgeted	Actual	Variance (£)	%
156	Wages (DL)	40,000	44,000	(4000)	(10)	120,000	114,000	6000	5	100,000	108,000	(8000)	(8)
1234	Raw Materials (DM)	560,000	565,600	(5600)	(1)	1,234,000	1,300,000	66,000	(5.4)	1,130,000	1,155,000	(25,000)	(2.2)

The significant variances need investigating and it is in the organisation's interest to define what significant means. Some organisations define significant if the variance (favourable or adverse) is above or below a defined percentage band. For example, if the band is 5% any variance above or below 5% will be investigated. Some organisations identify a certain sum of money.

FIXED AND FLEXIBLE BUDGETS

A fixed budget gives management information at the planning stage. This type of budget is quite rigid and cannot be adjusted to reflect the levels of activities that occur within the operational year. If the level of activity is significantly different there will be a significant volume of variances. The solution to the problem of variable levels of activity lies in the use of a flexible budget which is designed to change in accordance with the level of activity attained. All budgets are based on estimates so volumes of sales and production cannot be expected to conform exactly to the estimates of the fixed budget. So it is important to recognise that actual costs for the activity level should be compared with the expected costs for that level of activity — this means an organisation must compare like with like.

The flexible budget consists of not one budget, but of a series of budgets each being based on a different level of activity within the expected range (ie 70%, 80% or 90%).

Most organisations will, in practice, use a flexible budget for control purposes which is designed for adjustments to take place. The flexible budget recognises fixed, semi-variable and variable costs so the budget may be "flexed" to reflect the actual activity which is taking place.

Example

A company makes only one product which averages out on a monthly basis at 150,000 units. Levels of production may vary so the following budget has been prepared.

Figure 18 — Flexible Budget

Cost	Cost Behaviour	Budget £
Direct labour	Variable cost (£0.15 per unit)	22,500
Direct materials	Variable cost (£0.25 per unit)	37,500
Production overheads	Semi-variable £12,000+£0.10 per unit)	27,000
Administration overheads	Fixed	15,000
Total budgeted cost		102,000

Figure 19 — Budgets for 120,000 Units and 180,000 Units

	Flexed budget (120,000 units)	Flexed budget (150,000 units)	Flexed budget (180,000 units)
	£	£	£
Labour (£0.15 per unit)	18,000	22,500	27,000
Materials (£0.25 per unit)	30,000	37,500	45,000
Production overheads (£12,000 fixed + £0.10 per unit)	24,000	27,000	30,000
Administration overheads	15,000	15,000	15,000
Total	87,000	102,000	117,000

If the actual units produced per month were 130,000 then the actual costs must be compared with the budget prepared for that level.

Figure 20 — Budget for 130,000 Units

	Flexed budget (130,000 units)	Actual costs (130,000 units)	Variances + or (−)
	£	£	£
Labour (£0.15 per unit)	19,500	21,000	(1500)
Materials (£0.25 per unit)	32,500	30,600	1900
Production overheads (£12,000 fixed+£0.10 per unit)	25,000	25,700	(700)
Administration overheads	15,000	15,400	400
Total	92,000	92,700	(700)

It is by comparing like for like that management are able to use budgets as a credible means of control.

Cost Behaviour

The examples on flexible budgeting have been prepared on the basis of costs being fixed, semi-variable or variable in behaviour. Taking a closer look at this behaviour the following is important to take note of.

Fixed costs

These are costs which do not vary in total when output increases. An example of this is the price an organisation pays for rent and rates. No matter if one unit or a million units of production are produced the rent and rates will still be the same for the period under review.

Semi-variable costs

These are costs which have a proportion of fixed and variable costs in there make up. For example the charge on telephones is made up of a fixed rental line charge and a usage charge based upon how many telephone calls are made. These two components must be clearly identified and separated to give a clear identification for inclusion within total cost.

Variable costs

These are costs which vary in total, on a pro rata basis, as production increases or decreases. It is possible to express fixed costs and variable costs in graphic form.

Figure 21 — Fixed and Variable Costs

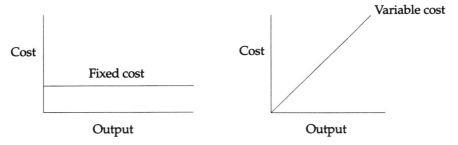

In normal circumstances fixed costs are indirect costs, but it is possible to have some variable overheads. Variable costs are mainly direct costs, but again it is possible to associate some of the variable costs with a fixed cost tag. An example of this would be when a workforce is on a guaranteed wage and is paid come rain or shine. For example deciding which telephone rental system a company should use. Telephone Company A charges a rental of £15 per line per quarter plus 30p for every unit consumed. Telephone Company B charges a rental of £20 per line per quarter, but only 20p a unit consumed. The interpretation of this graph shows that where the two lines cross we have a break-even point. Telephone Company A is the one to use if the units consumed are to be below 50. Above 50 units Company B is the one to use.

Figure 22 — Break-even Point

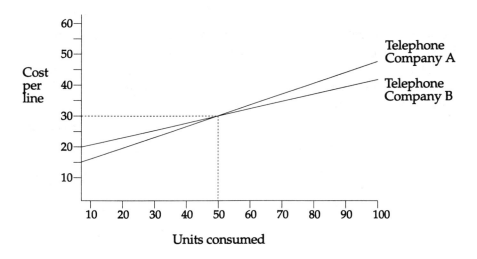

BREAK-EVEN ANALYSIS

Organisations use this technique to depict costs, sales revenue and output when the break-even point is the level of output where sales revenue equals costs. At this point the organisation is neither making a profit or a loss, ie it is at break-even point.

Example

An organisation makes a single product which it retails at £15. It has fixed costs of £100,000 pa and variables costs of £5 per unit. It has a maximum capacity of 20,000 units, but is only working at 75% of its operating capacity. From this information it is possible to show the following information.

The break-even point is at 10,000 units anything below this figure would be in a loss making capacity. Conversely, anything above this figure would give a profit. The margin of safety from break-even to operational capacity is 25% which means within this margin of between 50% and 75% operational capacity the organisation will still make a profit.

Figure 23 — Example of a Break-even Chart

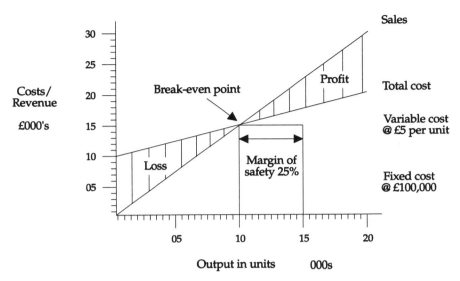

Contribution

This is the difference between sales value and variable costs and it is possible to refer to different products making a contribution towards fixed costs and profit. This means that an individual product contributes to the payment of fixed costs and the generation of profit.

sales – variable costs = contribution

contribution – fixed costs = profit

$$\text{break-even point in sales value} = \frac{\text{fixed costs} \times \text{sales}}{\text{contribution}}$$

Standard Costing (Control through Variances)

Standard costing is an extension of budgetary control, but the difference is that in standard costing a budget is prepared for each individual product or service. The objective is to set up predetermined standards of cost and other aspects of performance such as sales. The actual outcome can then be compared and variances between standard and actual can be computed. The setting up of standards is essential since they supply objective criteria against which performance can be measured.

Example

Standards must be realistic, attainable, agreed by operating personnel and regularly updated. If the standard cost of making a particular product is to be established then the material quantities must be evaluated by production personnel (ie the standard recipe), and prices established by purchasing personnel. Labour time must be evaluated by work study engineers and costed by wages staff. The premise in standard costing is that standards of performance should be achievable if machinery is operated efficiently, material properly used and appropriate allowances are made for normal losses, waste and machine downtime. The total cost variance is made up of the variances for each of the main elements of cost:

- materials
- labour
- overheads.

The variance for each element can be further analysed into a number of sub-variances which are used to identify the reasons for the variance. Once the reasons have been identified, the management of the business can take action to ensure that they do not happen again. The main variances and sub-variances for a manufacturing business are shown below.

Materials variances are:

- a price rise (or price fall) in the cost of materials
- a change in the amount of materials used.

Labour variances are:

- an unexpected rise in pay rates or the need to use a different grade of employee (at a higher or lower wage rate)
- a change in efficiency levels, ie a higher or lower output than expected.

Overhead variances are:

- an unexpected change in fixed costs, such as an increase in rent
- a change in the cost or use of a variable overhead, such as electricity.

The principle of variance analysis is that variances and sub-variances are identified and calculated until they can be seen to be the responsibility of an individual employee, or small section within the business.

Standard costs are, as we have already indicated, based upon a defined method, often worked out by work study techniques embracing total quality management systems, efficient working practices, quality materials and under good conditions. When production has taken place, or the service implemented, the actual costs of labour, material and overheads are recorded and any differences, called variances, between the standard cost and the actual cost, analysed to find the cause.

DECISION MAKING AND MARGINAL COSTING

Decision making means making a choice between alternatives in pursuit of specific, and where possible, quantifiable objectives. Rational decisions are based upon relevant information and are vested in the future. As the future is uncertain, decision making must cope with uncertainty.

Marginal Costing

Marginal costing is a decision making technique based on the principle that only variable costs (known also as marginal costs) change with output. As fixed costs do not alter they should be ignored when taking decisions affecting the level of activity.

Example

"The Bread Company" produce three main products — bread, morning goods and flour cakes. Product costs are ascertained using the absorption costing system which identifies the profit or loss of the products. There is a requirement to ascertain whether the bread production should be dropped from the product range in order to improve profitability.

Figure 24 — Example of Absorption Costing System

	Bread	*Morning goods*	*Flour cakes*	*TOTAL*
	£000s	*£000s*	*£000s*	*£000s*
Sales income	180	330	270	780
Less total costs	(200)	(250)	(220)	(670)
	(20)	80	50	110

It has been estimated that costs are 60% variable and 40% fixed

	Bread £000s	Morning goods £000s	Flour cakes £000s	TOTAL £000s
Total cost	200	250	220	670
Variable (60%)	120	150	132	402
Fixed (40%)	80	100	88	268

A re-drafting of the original statement is as follows.

	bread £000s	morning goods £000s	flour cakes £000s	TOTAL £000s
Sales income	180	330	270	780
Less variable costs	(120)	(150)	(132)	(402)
Contribution	60	180	138	378
Less fixed costs				(268)
Profit				110

The three products generate a contribution of £378,000 which is made up of fixed costs and profit. Products are judged on their contribution and not their profit. A product that generates a contribution, earns income in excess of its incremental cost and is therefore worth retaining. If the bread line was to be discontinued and was not replaced by any other new product the total contribution would be reduced to £318,000 and the profit margin by £60,000 to £50,000.

Example — pricing for special orders

"The Sandwich Bar" manufactures 1600 sandwiches (average and sales price of £1.25 per sandwich) generating a weekly income of £2000 from sandwiches. The costs of these sandwiches amount to £1600 which includes a fixed cost of £600. A local factory wishes to place an order for 400 sandwiches per week but at a reduction of 20% of the average price. Should "The Sandwich Bar" take the offer? In marginal costing systems:

contribution = sales income – variable costs

It can be seen that after the fixed costs have been covered, any special order can be appraised on its marginal costs. In this extra order the difference between sales and variable costs is a contribution of £150 which is also the profit margin because fixed costs have already been covered in normal production.

Figure 25 — Sample of Marginal Costing System

Normal	£	£ (per sandwich)	Extra	£	TOTAL (£)
Sales income	2000	1.25	400 × 1.00	400	2400
Less variable costs	1000	0.625	400 × 0.625	250	1250
Contribution	1000	0.625		150	1150
Less fixed costs	600	0.375			600
Profit	400	0.25		150	550

The Decision to Manufacture or Purchase

"The Bread Company" are considering whether to manufacture or purchase a new malted rye bread. The new malted rye bread comes in batches of 1000. The buying in price has been quoted at £0.55 and the marginal cost of manufacture is £0.43 per batch. The difficulty involved in this decision lies in the fact that to manufacture the rye bread the company would have to use up existing production capacity reducing the white batons manufacture by 200 units. The batons sell at 65p each and have a marginal cost of 40p each.

A decision has to be made as to whether "The Bread Company" manufacture the malted rye bread or buy.

Example — Cost Analysis of Batches of 1000 Malted Rye Bread

	£
Marginal cost of manufacture = £0.43 × 1000	430.00
Add the lost contribution for batons = 200 units x 0.25	50.00
Relevant manufacturing cost	480.00
Buying in 1000 units of malted rye bread = 1000 × 0.55	550.00

There is no gain in buying the rye bread, it is more profitable to manufacture.

In normal make or buy decisions the comparison is between the marginal cost of manufacture and the buying in price. In this example the lost contribution made from the batons was a relevant factor which had to be included in the analysis.

Stock Valuation — Total Costing (Absorption Costing) and Marginal Costing

Stocks at the end of a period are usually valued at either total production cost which includes both fixed and variable costs or at a marginal cost which does not include fixed costs. Using total costing some of the period's costs are transferred to the next period through stock valuation. In marginal costing all the fixed costs are charged to that period as only variable costs are transferred to the next period.

Example

In a period 80,000 units were produced and 72,000 sold, ie 8000 units of closing stock was left. The sales for the period amounted to £400,000 and the total production costs £200,000 made up of 70% variable cost and the rest fixed. General overheads were £50,000 fixed cost.

Using total costing:

price per unit =	total production cost	200,000	
	no of units produced	80,000	£2.50 per unit

closing stock valued = 8000 × £2.50 = £20,000

Using marginal costing:

price per unit =	marginal production cost	140,000	
	no of units produced	80,000	£1.75 per unit

closing stock valued = 8000 × £1.75 = £14,000

Operating Statement

Total Costing		£
Sales (72,000 × £5.00)	=	360,000
Less production cost		200,000
— closing stock	20,000	180,000
Gross Profit		180,000
Less general overheads		50,000
Net profit		130,000

Marginal Costing

		£
Sales (72,000 × £5.00)	=	360,000
Less marginal cost		140,000
— closing stock	14,000	126,000
	Contribution	234,000
Less Fixed costs	60,000	
General Overheads	50,000	110,000
Net Profit		124,000

The difference in the profits shown is due to the difference in stock valuation. The technique normally used for external accounting is absorption costing and it is probable that the technique will be used for internal reporting.

IN CONCLUSION

The information provided by management accounting can be provided in any format management chooses, so long as it fulfils its primary role of enabling management to run the enterprise as efficiently as possible.

The purposes of costing systems are to:

- make informed decisions
- plan and control
- ascertain stock valuations.

MAKING INFORMED DECISIONS

Costing provides vital information which helps management to make better decisions and pricing is one example of a decision which uses cost information. In this type of decision, a cost plus profit approach is often used to set the selling price of an enterprise's goods or services, or at least to set a marker for the selling price. Examples of other decisions which rely on cost information are:

- make or buy decisions (where an enterprise must decide whether to buy in components or to manufacture them itself)
- project evaluation (assessing the impact of a proposed project upon the enterprise in order to decide whether or not to proceed).

Pricing

To price accurately it is essential that relevant costing information is gathered and collected. The management accountant should liaise with all of the other managers who have a bearing on the pricing decision (eg production managers and marketing managers) for the purpose of gathering all the relevant information pertaining to the pricing decision at hand. His or her specialist skills are required to identify what costs are in fact relevant to the decision and also whether any information has been omitted or not. Once all of the relevant information has been collected, the management accountant should then present this information in as concise and easily understandable a form as possible to facilitate the decision making process.

To price a product or a service one of two methods will be used ie *absorption costing* or *marginal costing*.

Absorption costing is more suited to long-term pricing decisions, whereas marginal costing is suited to short-term pricing decisions.

Absorption Costing

This requires the calculation of the "total" or "full" cost of a product or service, which in turn requires the absorption of indirect costs (or overheads) into the individual units of product or service being costed. Once the total cost of a product or service has been established, this information can be used by management to help it in setting the selling price of the product or service in question. The total of the cost unit (ie the product or service) can assist management in the pricing decision by means of cost plus pricing which simply involves adding the required mark-up to the total to arrive at the selling price of the product or service.

Marginal Costing

In marginal costing only variable costs are charged to individual costs units. This involves establishing the variable costs of a cost unit and then setting a selling price which results in a total contribution being earned which is sufficient to pay for all the fixed costs of the enterprise leaving a balance representing the profits generated for the enterprise. "Contribution" has been defined as the difference between the selling price and variable cost of a cost unit.

Whichever of the above methods an enterprise uses to set the selling price of its products or services, the final price must also take account of other factors such as market conditions, ie the laws of supply and demand, competitor's prices and general economic indicators.

When are Marginal and Absorption Costing Used?

Retailers, generally, price their products using marginal costing (eg bought in price plus 33.33% mark-up). Marginal costing is used because of its simplicity and the fact that the volume of business is the main determinant of profit in the retail trade. Absorption costing would be difficult to implement given the wide range of products available and the difficulty of accurately predicting the volume of business.

Marginal costing is most suitable for a one-off order because it only takes into account the relevant costs of the order when setting the price of the order. If, however, one-off orders become too commonplace the enterprise may wish to consider using absorption costing to price the orders and thus ensure its fixed costs are covered.

An oil refinery would use absorption costing to price its products as this involves long-term production runs and the element of indirect costs in total costs would be too large to use marginal costing, which could ignore such costs in the pricing decision.

A government department would use absorption costing to justify its budget allocation. In the public sector, setting prices may not be appropriate as services are often given free to the public (that is if income tax is ignored) but absorption costing may still be used for planning and control purposes. If a public sector enterprise does need to set a price for its product or services, it would approach the decision in the same way as commercial enterprises. Public sector pricing is, however, the subject of more stringent social obligations, interference from politicians and consumer watchdogs than a commercial concern.

PLANNING AND CONTROL

The budgeting process of an enterprise is an example of planning and control. The planning element can only be worthwhile if the cost information on which it is based is reliable. Control is exercised by comparing actual performance to planned (or targeted) performance and analysing the differences.

When preparing the budgets of an enterprise, the objective is to end up with a master budget which quantifies the planned performance of the enterprise as a whole for the budget period. Before this can be put together the functional budgets must first be prepared. A "functional budget" is the budget of income or expenditure for a particular function of an enterprise (eg sales budget, production budget, manpower budget, etc).

All of these budgets are inter-related in that the preparation of one leads to another (eg you cannot prepare the production budget without first having a completed finished goods budget available on which to base the production schedules).

All enterprises are subject to at least one limiting factor. In most profit-seeking enterprises the limiting factor will be the level of sales the enterprise can achieve. In non-profit seeking enterprises the limiting factor is usually the level of resources which the enterprise has at its disposal. Budget preparation, in all cases, should begin with the preparation of the functional budget which incorporates the limiting factor. This is because all the other budgets of an enterprise must fit into the constraints set by the limiting factor.

Control of the budget is exercised by measuring the actual performance of the enterprise and by comparing these results with the budgeted performance. The results of this comparison then forms the basis of management decisions which will seek to correct adverse trends in the actual performance.

Some of the practical problems associated with implementing budgetary control include:

- setting realistic budgets in the first place
- finding a means of recording actual performance in a form suitable for comparison with the budget
- motivating managers to act upon the results of the comparison of actual and budgeted performance
- requires management to spend considerable time and commitment to the planning and monitoring of the budget.

Standing Costing

A "standing cost" is a predetermined estimate of the cost of a product or service (cost unit). Non-production overheads are generally omitted from the calculation of standard costs but can be included if their inclusion results in more meaningful cost information. The word "standard" is something that may be tested or measured. This definition supports the main purpose of a standard costing system which is the comparison of actual costs to standard costs. Any differences between the actual costs and predetermined standard costs (or revenues) is termed a "variance". These differences are then analysed by way of variance analysis to attempt to find the causes of the variances.

Standard costing and budgeting have a great deal in common. First, they both fulfil much the same roles in an enterprise. Second, both techniques exercise control by comparing actual results with expected results. The main difference between standard costing and budgeting is that standard costs are calculated per unit while budgets deal with the aggregate costs (eg total direct material costs in a budget).

Standard costing has two main advantages over budgeting.

1. Once standard costs have been established their application requires less clerical effort than with aggregate cost budgeting.

2. The comparison of actual results to standard can be performed quicker than with aggregate cost budgets. This arises because standard costs, which are calculated on a per unit basis, are automatically flexed.

Problems Associated with Standard Costing

The main problem with implementing a standard costing system in an enterprise is the calculation of the standard costs themselves. The calculation depends on the availability and accuracy of historical and forecasted data and the experience and judgement of managers. In practice, this data is not easy to obtain. If inaccurate "standards" are set, the purposes of implementing the costing system are defeated. This will result in a lot of wasted effort and money.

A second problem with standard costing is that it requires a "standard" product or service to cost in the first place (eg mass production of jam jars, oil refinery, automobiles, hairdressers, etc). If an enterprise's cost unit is not standard (eg custom built automobiles, kitchen units made to order, etc) then it is very difficult to calculate an average expected price per cost unit because each cost unit is different.

Most enterprises, especially those with homogeneous cost units, employ standard costing to some degree at least. It is usual that the standard setting process in such enterprises is an arduous one involving the review of past cost performance, forecasts of future levels of activity and cost behaviour and any other relevant information available. It is also likely that standard costs, once established, are the subject of ongoing review to ensure that they still apply in the specific circumstances of the enterprise. This review is necessary because of the dynamic environment in which most enterprises work today where the only constant is change. Any flaws in the standards themselves should also be revealed by the regular variance analysis. This takes place in a standard costing system and seeks explanations as to why actual performance differs from standard performance.

Stock Valuation

Stock valuation is required for inclusion in the periodic management and financial accounting profit and loss accounts and balance sheets of an enterprise. It is also required in the monitoring of stock levels and the investment therein (which is often substantial). The valuation of stocks is based on total production cost per unit.

GLOSSARY

absorption	By spreading the overheads of a cost centre over all the products passing through the cost centre it is possible to include all the overhead costs in the total cost of the product or service. The process by which this is equitably done is called overhead absorption or overhead recovery.
absorption costing of total cost	This is the term given to the method of finding product costs where total overheads are absorbed into production, based on the volume of production (expressed in labour or machine hours).
account balance	The difference between the debit and credit entries posted onto an account.
accounting concepts	Generally accepted assumptions that are used when preparing financial accounts.
accounting ratios	Ratios that are used to help analyse and interpret financial accounts.
accounting records	The books of account kept by a business which are used to record financial transactions.
accounting standards	Guidelines on how to deal with various accounting issues when preparing financial accounts.
appropriation account	Part of a limited company's profit and loss account. It shows how net profit (before tax) has been used, eg to pay tax or dividends.
assets	Items owned by a business. They are classed into fixed assets (eg land, equipment, motor vehicles) and current assets (eg stocks, trade debtors, cash balances held).
balance sheet	A statement of the financial position of a business at a given moment. It is a list of the business's assets and liabilities at a particular point in time.

bonus payment systems   The combination of a flat rate per hour with a bonus for achieving a given output.

break-even   The volume of sales which at the current gross margin produces just enough gross profit to cover the company's total overheads.

break-even analysis   A technique used to depict costs, sales revenue and output when the break-even point is the level of output where sales revenue equals cost.

budget   A plan is expressed in money. It is prepared and approved prior to the budget period and may show income, expenditure and the capital to be employed. It may be drawn up by showing incremental effects on former budgeted or actual figures or be compiled by zero based budgeting.

budgetary control   This is the establishment of budgets relating the responsibilities of executives to the requirements of a policy and the continuous comparison of actual budgeted results, either to secure by individual action the objectives of the policy or to provide a basis for its revision.

capital   The amount invested in a business by its owner(s). Capital employed is the money tied up in a business, ie how much the business is worth.

cash book   One of the books of account of a business. It is used to record bank and cash transactions.

coding   A system which ensures costs are charged correctly through the correct cost centres.

credit   A term used in relation to the double entry system. A credit is entered on the right hand side of an account and represents one of the two (dual) effects of a financial transaction.

continuous operation costing   This method is applicable where goods or services result from a sequence of continuous or repetitive operations or processes. Costs are averaged over the units produced during the period.

contribution This is the difference between sales value and variable costs and it is possible to refer to different products making a contribution towards fixed costs and profit. This means that an individual product contributes to the payment of fixed costs and the generation of profit.

corporate plan A detailed plan produced by an organisation's directors to show how they see the company developing. Once the corporate plan has been agreed by the Board of Directors it becomes the blueprint of what the directors expect the company to achieve over a given period of time in the future.

cost Describes the money spent on a particular item. Costing is the analysis of costs so that they can be allocated to products/services, activities, departments, and specific time periods.

cost apportionment The charging of proportions of each indirect or overhead cost item to cost centres using an appropriate basis of apportionment so as to reflect the relative use of that cost item by each cost centre.

cost behaviour The way costs behave on a fixed, semi-variable and variable basis.

Fixed costs are costs which do not vary in total when output increases.

Semi-variable costs are costs which have a proportion of fixed and variable costs in there make up.

Variable costs are costs which vary in total, on a pro rata basis, as production increases or decreases.

cost centre The cost centre can be a location (eg a production department) or a function (eg quality control)

day books Part of the books of account of a business. The sales day book is used to record credit sales. The purchase day book is used to record purchases made on a credit. These books can be used as part of the double entry system or may be part of a single entry system.

debit A term used in relation to the double entry system. A debit is entered on the left hand side of an account and represents one of the two (dual) effects of a financial transaction.

depreciation This is the decline in value, due to wear and the passage of time, of fixed assets. The *straight line method* reduces the value of an asset by an equal amount each year. The *reducing balance method* uses a predetermined percentage to write down the value of the asset in decreasing amounts. The amount of depreciation is charged each year and the percentage chosen will eventually write-off the asset over a number of years.

direct costs These make up the prime cost and can be allocated to the cost unit because they can easily be identified with it. They comprise of direct materials, direct labour and direct expenses.

double entry A system of book-keeping (recording transactions) that reflects the dual nature of financial transactions. For every single transaction, two entries are made in the accounting records.

financial accounting The production of (financial) accounts which show how a business has performed in financial terms. The two main items produced are the profit and loss account and the balance sheet.

fixed budget A fixed budget is prepared to give management generic information at the planning stage. This type of budget is quite rigid and cannot be adjusted to reflect the levels of activities that occur within the operational year.

flexible budget A flexible budget is designed for adjustments to take place. The flexible budget recognises fixed, semi-variable and variable costs so that the budget may be "flexed" to reflect the actual activity which is taking place.

gross profit   The difference between sales and the cost of the goods sold. The gross profit margin is a measure of the mark-up on the goods sold by a business.

indirect cost (or overhead)   Any cost which cannot be identified with a specific product or service is an indirect cost. Indirect costs, or overheads, have to be apportioned and then by a process known as absorption.

ledger   A collection of accounts or a storage place for the accounts maintained by a business. Individual accounts are used as part of the double entry system — each account is used to record similar transactions, eg all payments of rent will be recorded in the rent account. There are three main types of ledger — the sales, purchase and nominal ledgers.

liabilities   What the business owes. They are classed into current (due for payment in the next year) and long term (due for payment after one year). Examples of current liabilities are trade creditors, accruals and bank overdraft. A typical long liability is a five year bank loan.

limited company   A business with its own legal identity and a limit on the liability of its owners (in relation to any debts of the company) is limited to the amount due on any unpaid shares held. A plc can offer its shares for sale to the public whereas a private company cannot.

management accounting   Concerned with providing the management with financial information which will help with decision-making, planning and control. Typical documents produced are budgets and cash flows.

marginal costing   Marginal costing is a decision-making technique based on the principle only variable costs (known also as marginal costs) change with output. As fixed costs do not alter they should be ignored when taking decisions affecting the level of activity.

material valuation
The valuation of material by FIFO, LIFO standard cost or weighted average.

net profit
Gross profit less expenses. This is the profit when all costs have been taken into consideration — sometimes called the "bottom line" figure.

partnership
A business which is run by two or more people — the partners. The partners are personally responsible for the business's debts.

piecework
This is paid on the basis of an agreed rate per unit or operation for the number of units produced or operation carried out.

prime costs
The sum total of direct costs.

profit and loss account
Strictly speaking the trading and profit and loss account. It measures the amount of profit or loss made by a business over a time period.

profit centre
A profit centre is part of a business accountable for costs and revenues.

share capital
Consists of authorised and issued share capital. Authorised share capital is the amount of shares the company is allowed to issue in order to raise funds. Issued share capital is the amount of shares actually issued and taken up. Only limited companies have share capital — it never appears in the accounts of sole traders or partnerships.

single entry
A system of keeping books where only one entry is made per financial transaction. An example of a set of single entry records would be day books and a cash book.

sole trader
An individual person running a business. The business is owned by the sole trader who is responsible for all of its debts.

specific order costings

This is the basic cost accounting method applicable where work consists of separate contracts, jobs or batches. In specific order costing all the direct costs are charged to the cost unit and overheads are charged to the cost centres and then absorbed according to the time taken.

standard costing (control through variances)

Standard costing is an extension of budgetary control but the difference is that in standard costing a budget is prepared for each individual product or service. The objective is to set up predetermined standards of cost and other aspects of performance such as sales. The actual outcome can then be compared and variances between standard and actual can be computed.

trial balance

A list of all the balances on all of the accounts kept by the business. There will be debit and credit balances and if the trial balance is to "balance" then the debits exactly equal the credits. The trial balance can be used to produced the profit and loss account, and the balance sheet.

under absorption and over absorption

At the end of an accounting period, adjustments are made which take into account the actual overheads and the difference between the estimated figures. If the overheads absorbed by production are greater than the actual overheads this is known as over absorption and conversely if under the actual figure it is known as under absorption.

INDEX

A

B

C

Q

R

W

Z